IN
Taylor Nation

TRUE ENCOUNTERS WITH TAYLOR SWIFT

BY SARAH OLIVER

LESSER GODS

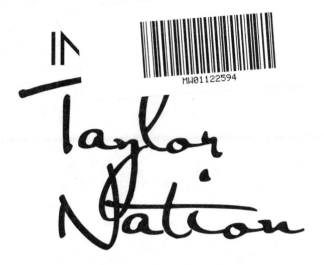

FIRST PUBLISHED IN THE UNITED STATES OF AMERICA IN 2016 BY:
Lesser Gods, 15 W. 36th St., 8th Fl., New York, NY 10018,
an imprint of Overamstel Publishers, Inc.
PHONE (646) 850-4201
www.lessergodsbooks.com

Originally published in the United Kingdom as *Taylor Swift: Everything Has Changed* by John Blake Publishing Ltd in 2016

DISTRIBUTED BY: Consortium Book Sales & Distribution,
34 13th Ave. NE #101, Minneapolis, MN 55413
PHONE (800) 283-3572
www.cbsd.com

FIRST U.S. EDITION September 2016 / 10 9 8 7 6 5 4 3 2 1
PRINTED AND BOUND IN THE U.S.A.
ISBN: 978-1-944713-05-8
LIBRARY OF CONGRESS CONTROL NUMBER: 2016939178

Dedicated with love to my cousin, Tom Durbin, and his bride-to-be, Lizzi Albert.

TABLE OF CONTENTS

CHAPTER 1

TAYLOR'S FAMILY AND FRIENDS

Before you start reading the stories contained in this book, it's a good idea to familiarize yourself with the people who make up Taylor's family and friends.

MAMA AND PAPA SWIFT

Many people who know the Swift family well say that Taylor has inherited her mom's strength and passion for work and family. Her mom isn't very musical herself—she was working as a marketing manager in an advertising agency when she met Taylor's dad—but her own mom (Taylor's grandmother) was an opera singer.

Andrea and Scott have been happily married for over twenty five years. They married in Texas on February 20, 1988 and settled in West Reading in Berks County, Pennsylvania. Scott is a very intelligent man and has spent his working life in the finance world, following in the footsteps of his own father and grandfather. Taylor is very proud of her stockbroker dad and looks to him for financial advice. She says he's as passionate about finance as she is about music!

Taylor was born on December 13,1989 at 8:36 a.m. at Brampton Civic Hospital. Andrea and Scott chose a gender neutral first name for their baby girl in case she grew up to work in finance like her daddy, as no one would be able to tell whether she was a man or a woman from her business cards. They chose Alison for Taylor's middle name, after her aunt.

Taylor is super close to her mom Andrea, a woman Swifties affectionately call "Mama Swift." In February 2008 she told the *Washington Post*: "I know I'm so lucky that I got two perfect parents, you know? I'm really good friends with [American country music artist and TV personality] Kellie [Pickler], whose mom abandoned her. I look at my mom, who's been there for everything, and I think, like, if I'd been in Kellie's situation, I probably wouldn't have made it. I look at other people who have absentee fathers or self-consumed mothers and I'm so lucky.

"My mom is my best friend. She's been there for me when no one else has. And she's never been afraid of telling me the honest truth. I think it's great to have somebody around who isn't afraid of hurting your feelings. She sat me down before the CMA Awards and said: 'You're not going to win this one. You're on a tiny label and if you win this, it's a miracle.' She was being realistic with me. So I went in with the attitude that it was just great to be nominated. And when I won, it made it that much sweeter. She talks to me like that, but she'll also build me up. I respect her so much. My dad is just a big teddy bear, who tells me that everything I do is perfect."

She summed up just how much her family mean to her in the song, "The Best Day," from her second album, *Fearless*. It's a sweet song, with Taylor remembering the wonderful childhood she had, thanks to her parents. She also sings about one of the worst experiences of her life from when she was thirteen years old. She'd asked some friends from school if they wanted to go to the mall but they said they were too busy, only for Taylor to visit the mall with her mom and see them there. Andrea drove her to another mall that was ninety minutes away so they could still have a nice day and she helped put a smile back on Taylor's face.

"The Best Day" might have been dedicated to her mom, but Taylor also sang about her "excellent father," whose "strength is making me stronger," and her younger brother Austin, who "inside and out" is "better than I am."

Taylor wrote the song one summer but kept it a secret from her mom until a few months later. Andrea revealed what happened in an interview with the TV show *Dateline*. She said: "The first time that she played 'The Best Day' for me was Christmas Eve. She had made this edited music video. I'm looking on the TV and this video comes up with this voice that sounds exactly like Taylor's. And I looked over at her and she said, 'I wrote it for you, Mom.' And that's when I lost it. And I've lost it pretty much every time I've heard that song since."

Andrea and Scott are extremely proud of their daughter and all that she has achieved. Taylor is a well-rounded young woman and will always put her family and fans first. When she turned eighteen on December 13, 2007, they threw her a pink-themed party. Her mom told *People* magazine at the time: "This party is our birthday gift to her. She knows the real gifts in life are relationships."

Taylor had a lovely time at the party and when asked by *People* magazine what the best part of turning eighteen was, she said: "I wanted a number one record, and I got that. And I got something I didn't even ask for, a Grammy nomination."

A year later, she had another party, inviting forty of her closest friends and family members into her home to help celebrate the last year of her teens. They enjoyed a relaxed evening, feasting on mini beef Wellingtons, scallops and sushi, and taking part in a Ping-Pong tournament. The winner was Taylor's manager, although Taylor also did well—she made the semi-finals. Afterward, they watched a movie that Taylor had made and enjoyed some s'mores by a fire pit in her garden. Taylor hadn't wanted lots of expensive gifts for her birthday, asking instead for some stationery and a new pair of glasses from her parents because hers had recently broken and she'd been taping them together. This sums up Taylor perfectly: she might be one of the most in-demand singers on the planet but at heart she's just a normal girl, who isn't materialistic at all and likes the simple things in life.

Taylor gets her down-to-earth nature from her mom. Superfan Jencita Vargas summed up just how special Mama Swift is in a post on the fansite, TT4Taylor. She said: "Andrea, more affectionately known as Mama Swift, has become a huge and important part of so many lives. She's a mother to those who have none; she's a friend to those who need one. She's an excellent listener, a fine baker—and have you tried her candied bacon?! I haven't, but it is all the rage, according to everyone who has been at a get-together with her!

"If you've had the pleasure of meeting her, you will recount the special moments shared together. She will walk right up to you and instantly make you feel comfortable. She will ask you to get a picture with her, so you don't have to awkwardly ask. She will give you a big hug and thank you for coming to see her daughter."

When Taylor revealed that her mom was battling cancer in April 2015, fans around the world were shocked but instantly started praying. Taylor wrote in a post on Tumblr:

> Hey guys,
>
> I'm writing to you with an update I wish I wasn't giving you, but it's important and I'm used to sharing important events in my life with you. Usually when things happen to me, I process them and then write music about how I feel, and you hear it much later. This is something my family and I thought you should know about now.
>
> For Christmas this year, I asked my mom that one of her gifts to me be her going to the doctor to get screened for any health issues, just to ease some worries of mine. She agreed, and went in to get checked. There were no red flags and she felt perfectly fine, but she did it just to get me and my brother off her case about it.
>
> The results came in, and I'm saddened to tell you that my mom has been diagnosed with cancer. I'd like to keep

the details of her condition and treatment plans private, but she wanted you to know.

She wanted you to know because your parents may be too busy juggling everything they've got going on to go to the doctor, and maybe you reminding them to go get checked for cancer could possibly lead to an early diagnosis and an easier battle . . . Or peace of mind in knowing that they're healthy and there's nothing to worry about. She wanted you to know why she may not be at as many shows this tour. She's got an important battle to fight.

Thank you for caring about my family so much that she would want me to share this information with you.

I hope and pray that you never get news like this.

Love you.

Taylor

The Swift family will always be upfront and honest with Taylor's fans as they see them as part of their extended family.

AUSTIN

On March 4, 1993, when Taylor was two-and-a-half years old, her brother Austin was born. They have a great relationship, although they don't see each other as much as they'd like because of Taylor's busy tour schedule and Austin away at college.

Austin is a student at Vanderbilt University in Nashville, Tennessee, and does freelance photography in his spare time. He actually photographed Taylor for a 2009 behind-the-scenes article in *People* magazine and he's also photographed her for *Rolling Stone* magazine.

When Taylor won three American Music Awards in November 2011 she was so glad that Austin was there to support her that she thanked him in one of her acceptance speeches. She told *Access Hollywood* afterward: "It really was wonderful that my brother was here to see that.

"He's usually at college. He goes to college and just lives a completely different life than me. To take him into my world for a second, it made me feel really good to be winning."

Taylor also brought Austin as her date to the *2015 MTV Video Music Awards* on August 30. That night she picked up three awards and later they partied at the Republic Records VMA After Party. Taylor's friend and "Royals" hitmaker Lorde was there and overheard a conversation between the two siblings. She shared over Twitter: "At the after party austin leaned down from the banquette heaving with models in vip to whisper in taylor's ear 'we grew up on a FARM!!' "

Taylor saw the tweet and decided to post her own, sharing with her followers a cute photo of Austin and herself as small children with their dad on a tractor.

BRITANY MAACK

When Taylor lived in Pennsylvania, her best friend was a girl called Britany Maack. They first met when they were a couple of months old, and as they grew up together both girls developed a love for horses and horse riding. They would spend as much time with each other as they could and would try to ignore the haters who thought they were uncool simply because they didn't want to get drunk.

Britany told the *Reading Eagle* in 2011: "We were more sisters than friends. Taylor's family was my family.

"In the summer our parents would go to the beach and I always remember going to her house in Stone Harbor. Her parents would take us on boat and jet-ski rides and we would play all day long in that bayside house.

"Taylor is still as imaginative as she was as a little girl. She was always extremely smart growing up. She looked at things almost with what I would call an old soul, but she also had an amazing imagination. Taylor is very similar to who she was years ago."

Britany loves seeing Taylor perform live, and when they get the chance to catch up it always feels like they've never been apart. Taylor regularly posts photos of their get-togethers on Instagram, as well as embarrassing pictures of the two of them when they were growing up.

When she got engaged in early 2015, Britany knew there was only one person who could be her maid of honor—Taylor. She sent Taylor a framed photo of the two of them dressed up for Halloween when they were around four or five years old and a card that read: "Taylor, you are more than a friend, you are more than a best friend, you are my sister. I cannot imagine having anyone else by my side on my wedding day . . . will you be my maid of honor?" Taylor shared a photo of the card and childhood snap on Instagram with the message "Yeah I will @ brittmaack."

A few months later Taylor and Britany had a great time shopping for a wedding dress, with Taylor telling *People* magazine: "I've never been a maid of honor before. This is my first time, and it's really, really important to me because this is my best friend, who I've known since I was born. And she's marrying someone I've known since I was four."

The pair visited the Reem Acra showroom in New York, " . . . because that's one of her (and my) favorite designers. Reem does the most amazing bridal designs, and Britany and I were looking through *Vogue*, and she pointed to this one gown, and I was like, 'I wonder if we could go to the showroom?' "

ABIGAIL ANDERSON

Taylor might have been sad to leave Britany behind when she was fourteen and moved to Tennessee, but she did make new friends. On her first day at her new school she sat next to a girl called Abigail Anderson in English class and they soon became inseparable. Taylor might have dreamed about becoming a performer but for Abigail it wasn't the stage that was calling her, but the swimming pool: she really wanted to become a professional swimmer.

The two girls loved reading and one of the books they studied in their English class was Harper Lee's classic, *To Kill a Mockingbird*. Taylor was really inspired by the novel, telling Big Machine Label Group: "You know, you hear storytelling, like in Harper Lee's *To Kill a Mockingbird*, and it just . . . it makes your mind wander. It makes you feel like it makes your world more vast. And you think about more things and greater concepts after you read something like that."

When Taylor became famous after her first album was released in 2006, she and Abigail didn't let it affect their friendship; in fact, Abigail was behind her one hundred percent. At first, Taylor remained in school, but eventually she had to leave and be home-schooled instead. She was gutted she wouldn't see Abigail every day but they still met up as often as they could. Taylor told *Billboard* in March 2008: "Balancing all this [school work and music] is not hard. I mean, what do I have to complain about? I have the best time in the world. I'm so lucky. When I go out in public and I go to a mall, yeah, it's a lot different than it was two years ago, but it's a beautiful kind of different. It's the kind of different that I've wanted my entire life. I'm a strong believer that if you work your entire life for something, and you work so hard and you want this one thing so much, you should never complain once you get it."

Abigail openly admits that it was tough when Taylor left school, telling the *Lawrence Journal-World* newspaper: "I mean, any girl knows that if your best friend leaves you in tenth grade, it's just like, 'Okay, what do I do now?' So, it was hard for both of us.

"I had to kind of make a new name for myself around school, and she had to do her own thing out there and miss everything that had been her life for the previous few years. But she just immediately started doing so well . . . you just couldn't really think about anything else."

Rather than relax during summer vacation like her peers, Taylor had to work harder than she'd ever worked before: she had her first radio tour. She tried to visit 2,500 stations to encourage them to play her music. Her manager at the time, Rick Barker, had given her a simple piece of advice: if you want to sell 500,000 records, then you should aim to meet 500,000 people.

Andrea was really supportive and volunteered to do the driving. They slept in their car and handed out homemade cookies to people who worked at the radio stations to add a personal touch. Taylor and her mom found the tour very tiring, but they had fun too—it was a big adventure.

Every time a radio station played her single, Taylor sent them a personal handwritten note to thank them. Taylor and Andrea's hard work paid off and her first single, "Tim McGraw," reached number six on the *Billboard* Hot Country Songs chart; it was in the top ten for thirty-five weeks.

Taylor says she'll always remember where she was when she heard "Tim McGraw" being played for the first time. She revealed to *Seventeen* magazine: "I was driving down the road and somebody called in and requested it, and I almost drove off the road—literally.

"My record label president still has the message of me screaming at the top of my lungs, screeching; you can barely hear what I'm saying because I was crying—it was amazing."

When Taylor's second album, *Fearless*, was about to be released, talk show host Ellen DeGeneres flew Abigail Anderson in for the release party—with Justin Timberlake.

The song on the album that Taylor was most proud of was "Fifteen," a track that had been inspired by a horrible break-up experience of Abigail's. Her friend liked the track too and didn't mind Taylor telling the world what had happened to her. Taylor felt that "Fifteen" was the best song she'd written up to this point in her career. In the emotional track she offers advice to other girls facing their freshman year. She told the website PopMatters: "It says, 'I should have known this,

I didn't know that, here's what I learned, here's what I still don't know.' It took me a really long time to figure out how I was going to tell all these different stories about meeting my best friend and watching her get her heart ripped out, and me having to choose a career over a boy."

When it came to recording the track for her album, Taylor cried because she found it so emotional. She couldn't stop thinking about the pain Abigail had suffered because of the breakup.

DID YOU KNOW?

As well as appearing in the video for "Fifteen," Abigail also appears in the videos for "Teardrops On My Guitar," "Picture To Burn," "I'm Only Me When I'm With You" and "22."

Taylor was super excited when she graduated from high school in the summer of 2008 because it had taken a lot of effort on her part to keep up with her studies. She told *People* magazine at the time: "It's really good to know you don't have to give up on your dreams to graduate high school, and you don't have to quit your education to live your dreams. It's really cool that you can do both."

Taylor has continued to value Abigail's friendship and she took her to the 2015 Grammys as her date. The pair love vacationing together whenever they can and share photos on Instagram. Abigail's account is abigail_lauren, so why not check out her latest photos?

SCOTT BORCHETTA

Swifties have a lot to thank Scott Borchetta for: he was the music executive who discovered Taylor and signed her to his record label.

Scott has been in the music industry his entire working life. He had been employed by Universal Music Group, running their DreamWorks Nashville division until it was shut down in 2005. Having decided he would set up his own record label, he now needed to find a new star.

One night, he went to the famous Bluebird Café to see their showcase, a regular event where singer-songwriters hoping to be discovered sing their hearts out to an audience made up of music industry people like Scott. It was here that, among others, country singers Garth Brooks, Ashley Cleveland and Pam Tillis were discovered.

Scott had met Taylor briefly while he was at DreamWorks Nashville, but nothing could have prepared him for her performance that night. Quite literally, she took his breath away. He confessed to *Billboard*: "When I met her, I was just smitten. She was a fascinating person, even at fourteen years old. She had such an amazing desire for people to like her and get to know her, and she has found a way to engage anybody whom she wants to, whether it's the immediate fan or the biggest stars in the world."

As soon as the show finished, Scott arranged to meet Taylor and her parents. He told them that he wanted to sign her to a record deal but he would need her to wait for him as he was no longer with Universal and was in the process of setting up his own label. He knew that Taylor was really special after he heard her sing "Tim McGraw."

Taylor and her parents had faith in Scott and he left telling his friends in the music industry that he'd found the next big thing. Soon afterwards he launched Big Machine Records and Taylor was officially signed up. Scott wanted his label to be different: he wanted to put the music and the artist first.

In those early days, Taylor was just as passionate about her fans as she is today. She spent lots of time on Myspace, building a profile she was proud of. Before meeting Scott, she already had a website, confessing in 2008 to Reuters: "I was, like, twelve when we secured taylorswift.com and started putting up different versions of a website" And when we moved to Nashville, my mom and I got really proactive with trying to make it really, really cool. We went to Mad Dancer Media, and we told them we wanted it to look like a scrapbook. And there are all these buttons on it and it opens the book, and there are all these tabs and pages, and we wanted it to be really interactive and really appropriate for where I was in my life at that point. I didn't want a sleek, too cool site. I wanted it to be reflective of who I was as a person and who I am as a person. And that's kind of casual.

"I spend so much time on Myspace. It's the best way to figure out what your fans and what your friends and these people that helped you get where you are, what they're going through and what they want to hear from you, what they're liking, what they're not. My Myspace [page] is something that I made. The background that you see on there, I went to a website and copied the code and copy-and-pasted my "about me" section. I upload all the pictures, I check the comments, I am in charge of everything on that page. It really is important to me and really special to me when someone comes up to me and says, 'I'm your friend on Myspace.' I've always taken so much pride in it just because it's really personal to me."

As Taylor's fame grew, Scott wanted to protect her and to make sure that she didn't burn out. He was keen for her to have a long, successful career and he didn't want her to feel she was under any pressure at all. Today, she considers him a good friend and is so glad that he was in the audience that night when she sang in the Bluebird Café: he made her dreams come true.

LIZ ROSE

Over the years, songwriter Liz Rose has become Taylor's right-hand woman. They have been writing together since 2006 and Liz cowrote some of Taylor's biggest hits, including "Teardrops on My Guitar" and "White Horse." Liz has always respected Taylor, even when she was still at school; they used to meet for two hours every Tuesday to write together. She has always valued Taylor's opinion and let her write what she wanted to write—just helping her along the way. Liz talked about their early days to *Blender* magazine: "Basically, I was just her editor. She'd write about what happened in school that day. She had such a clear vision of what she was trying to say. And she'd come in with the most incredible hooks."

When Taylor was thirteen she secured an artist development deal with RCA Records. Sony thought she was a talented songwriter and they wanted her to write some songs for some of their other artists. She became the youngest staff songwriter they'd ever had. Although RCA records thought Taylor had huge potential, they weren't willing to let her release an album herself until she was eighteen. This was a real blow to Taylor and her family.

Taylor didn't think waiting was the right thing to do, so she decided to walk away from RCA even though it was a risky move. She also instructed Sony not to sell her songs because she was going to be singing them herself. This all happened shortly after Taylor had been with RCA for a year and she'd performed some of her best songs to the big bosses. She explained what happened to journalist John Preston from the *Telegraph*: "Basically, there were three things that were going to happen. Either they were going to drop me, or shelve me—that's kind of like putting me in cold storage—or give me a record deal. Of course, the only one of those that you want is the record deal. But they announced they were going to shelve me, and 'monitor my progress' until I was eighteen.

"[I was devastated]—I mean, I was fourteen. I genuinely felt that I was running out of time. I'd written all these songs and I wanted to capture these years of my life on an album while they still represented what I was going through."

Taylor's brave move paid off—she was soon discovered by Scott Borchetta and the rest is history. She still got to work with Liz Rose, and it was she who helped Taylor shape "Tim McGraw" into the song we all know and love. Taylor had first come up with the melody and some lyrics in math class. She worked at it at home after school, added some piano melody and then took it to Liz to find out what she thought of it. Together, they finished shaping it.

DID YOU KNOW?

It's thought that the inspiration for the song "Tim McGraw" was Taylor's ex-boyfriend Brandon Borello, a senior at her school.

Taylor has always liked to use real-life experiences when writing songs. She told the *Washington Post* that she could "draw inspiration from anything . . . if you're a good storyteller, you can take a dirty look somebody gives you, or if a guy you used to have flirtations with starts dating a new girl or somebody you're casually talking to says something that makes you sooooo mad—you can create an entire scenario around that."

When she wrote "Teardrops On My Guitar" with Liz Rose, she based it on her feelings for a guy called Drew Hardwick. She explained to the *Country Standard Times*: "[He] would sit there every day talking to me about another girl: how beautiful she was, how nice and how smart and perfect she was."

Taylor would do her best to hide how this made her feel, give him a fake smile and wonder if he knew she was thinking of him every night. She came up with the idea to use this experience as the basis for a song while making her way home from school one day.

On her self-titled first album, Taylor wrote the following songs with Liz Rose: "Tim McGraw," "Picture To Burn," "Teardrops On My Guitar," "Cold as You," "Tied Together With A Smile," "Stay Beautiful" and "Mary's Song (Oh My My My)." She wrote "A Place In This World" with Robert Ellis

Orrall and Angelo Petraglia and "The Outside," "Should've Said No" and "Our Song" on her own.

Liz really understood who Taylor wanted to be as an artist and together they worked together again on her second album, *Fearless*. They wrote "Tell Me Why" after Taylor arrived at a writing session angry about a guy and Liz asked what she would say to him if she could. Taylor admitted she would say that she was sick and tired of his attitude and that she felt she didn't even know him. As she let it all off her chest, Liz started writing it down and soon they had the beginnings of a song that would become "Tell Me Why."

On her *Fearless* album, Liz and Taylor wrote the title track "Fearless," "White Horse," "You Belong With Me," "Tell Me Why," "Come In With The Rain" and "Superstar" together. Taylor wrote "Breathe" with Colbie Caillat, "The Way I Love You" with John Rich, and "Untouchable" with Cary Barlowe, Nathan Barlowe and Tommy Lee James. The other tracks, Taylor wrote by herself: "Fifteen," "Love Story," "Hey Stephen," "You're Not Sorry," "Forever & Always," "The Best Day," "Change" and "The Other Side Of The Door."

In an interview with Carla Hay from Examiner.com, Taylor explained why she decided to call the album *Fearless*. She said: "It's a big deal to title your album, so I wanted to make sure that it was the right call. I started thinking about the word 'fearless,' and what it means to me. It isn't that you're completely unafraid. I think fearless is having fears, but jumping anyway."

She wrote many of the songs while touring, adding: "All the songs for the second record, it's like they were already produced in my head. When I was writing a song, I knew what every instrument was doing. The strings, mandolin, banjo or dobro [a resonator guitar], I heard it all. It was just really cool to have all those instruments I heard end up on my album."

The album very nearly didn't have "Forever & Always" on it, but Taylor pulled out all the stops to include it in the platinum edition. In the process she might have stressed out some people at her label, but she didn't mind. She confessed to *Rolling Stone*: "I think that it's fun making an album, knowing that two days before you're scheduled to have the last master in, and everything finished, and they're about to go print up the booklets, I can write something, call up my producer, we can get in the studio, put a rush on it, get an overnight mix, and that can be a last-minute addition to the record. I've had that happen on both my first and second albums, the last-minute, eleventh-hour songs.

"The two songs that were completely last-minute were, on the first record, 'Should Have Said No,' and on the second album, 'Forever & Always.' Both of them had to do with something really, really dramatic and crazy happening to me and me needing to address it in the form of music."

DID YOU KNOW?

Most songs only take Taylor thirty minutes or so to write. She wrote "Love Story" when she was lying on her bedroom floor—and it only took her twenty minutes!

Fearless was released on November 11, 2008. Taylor made a special appearance at a local store at midnight on the 10th to meet some of her most devoted fans. She didn't have much time to sleep as she was appearing on *Good Morning America*, just as she had on the day of her first album's release. She promoted the album as much as she could, and it paid off: in the first week she sold ten times more copies than her first album had in its first week and it topped the charts!

For her third album, *Speak Now*, Taylor wrote all the songs single-handedly, so she didn't work on it with Liz Rose, but their track "All Too Well" was included on her fourth album, *Red*.

The song tells the story of a broken relationship. Taylor remembers what it was like to dance in the kitchen and go on road trips, to flick through a photo album with her boyfriend's mom only for the relationship to end and to receive her belongings back in the mail. It was the first song she had written in six months and she needed her friend Liz to help her finish it. She confessed to news anchor Katie Couric: "I was going through something that was so hard it was almost stifling, and so I wrote all these verses about everything from beginning to end of this relationship, and it ended up being, like, a ten-minute song."

Together, Liz and Taylor managed to cut the song down to five minutes and twenty-nine seconds. It's a very honest song, widely believed to be about her relationship with actor Jake Gyllenhaal.

NATHAN CHAPMAN

Back in the early days, award-winning record producer Nathan Chapman helped Taylor record her demos. Chapman had never produced a full album before, but he had plenty of talent and had been looking for his big break. Taylor really liked working with him and was thrilled when he got the thumbs-up to produce her first album.

She explained to CMT News: "We switched [album] producers a bunch of times [in the beginning]. I started off with this demo producer who worked in a little shed behind this publishing company I was at. His name was Nathan Chapman. I'd always go in there and play him some new songs, and the next week he would have this awesome track, on which he played every instrument, and it sounded like a record. We did this for a period of a year to two years before I got my record deal.

"Then, all of a sudden, it was, 'Okay, we're going to use this producer,' or 'We're going to use that producer.' So I got to record with a bunch of really awesome producers in Nashville. But it didn't sound the way it did with Nathan. He had never made an album before. He had just recorded demos. But the right chemistry hit. Finally my record label president said, 'Okay, try some sides with Nathan.' "

Nathan understood how involved Taylor likes to get in the studio and together they worked as a team to create the best album they could. She continued: "When I write a song, I hear how it is supposed to sound in my head. I can hear the production. I can hear what the drums are doing, what the mandolin is doing, what the bass is doing, when I'm writing that song. So usually, when we go to the studio, all I have to do is sit down with Nathan for ten minutes and say, 'This is how I want this to sound,' and he [brings] it all to life."

Taylor was impressed with what they managed to produce after four months of hard work. She told MTV in 2011: "I look back on the record I made when I was sixteen, and I'm so happy I made it. I got to immortalize those emotions that when you're so angry you hate everything. It's like recording your diary over the years, and that's a gift."

The album was released on October 24, 2006, a day she will never forget. Taylor was due to perform on *Good Morning America* but was so nervous she woke up in her hotel room at 5:00 a.m. Later that morning, she told them: "I just want to do that and put it on the register face down. I can't even express how excited/nervous I am. It's such a cool day, because I am in New York City and it feels like that's the place where your album should be released."

Music critics across the US, and around the world, thought her first album was great and wrote glowing reviews. Jeff Tamarkin wrote in his review for *All Music*: "That Swift is a talent to be reckoned with is never in doubt: her delivery on tracks like the uptempo 'The Outside,' the spare acoustic ballad 'Mary's Song (Oh My My My),' and especially the leadoff track 'Tim McGraw,' which was the first single from the album, is that of a seasoned pro, despite Swift's newcomer status. 'Tim McGraw' may also be the album's highlight—not a teenager's tribute to the country superstar, it instead uses McGraw as a marker in a lover's timeline: 'When you think Tim McGraw/ I hope you think my favorite song.' It's a device that's been used countless times in as many ways, that of associating a failed affair with items, places, and people, yet it works as a hook here and manages to come off as an original idea."

Rick Bell was equally as impressed, writing in his review for *Country Standard Time*: "Swift wrote or co-wrote all the cuts, but credits her coauthors—primarily Liz Rose, who pitched in on seven songs, including 'Tim McGraw'—for lending direction and focus. Swift's best efforts come on her deeply personal, self-penned songs, particularly 'The Outside' and 'Our Song,' which she sings with stirring conviction. It's an impressive debut that, while she pines about lost love and Tim McGraw, will likely have others singing the praises of Taylor Swift."

Taylor's fan base grew and grew as more and more people bought her record and appreciated her honest, autobiographical songs. It debuted at Number 19 on the *Billboard* 200 chart and peaked at Number 5—a fantastic achievement.

She was thrilled when the album earned gold certification after selling 500,000 copies, since this was the benchmark she set herself in the beginning when she started her six-month-long radio tour. A few months later, she had more reason to celebrate as she won her first big music award, the Breakthrough Video of the Year, for "Tim McGraw" at the CMT Music Awards.

When Taylor was invited to perform at huge events like the Academy of Country Music Awards and the Country Music Festival it made her happy because she loved having the opportunity to perform in front of country greats like Tim McGraw himself, Brad Paisley, Keith Urban and Kellie Pickler.

On her blog she compared her visit to the festival as a performer with her previous two visits. She wrote: "I went the first year as a volunteer (when I was fourteen) and helped out with getting artists to their radio interviews. The last year, I was there signing autographs (nobody knew who I was, it was funny) and telling anyone who would listen that I had a single coming out called 'Tim McGraw' and would they please request it [on the] radio . . . ha-ha. Then, one year later, there I was, receiving a platinum plaque for a million copies of my album sold. It's been a good year."

When the album topped the *Billboard* Country Album chart both Taylor and her producer Nathan Chapman were over the moon, not to mention her family, Scott Borchetta, Liz Rose and everyone else who worked on it. They didn't have time to slow down, though, as they wanted her second album to be even better. *Fearless* would actually go on to earn them a Grammy for Best Album at the 2010 ceremony as they co-produced it.

Nathan explained to MusicRadar how it felt to win: "It was cool to have something like that happen early in my career. It let me see how high the bar is. But winning the Grammy didn't take away my dreams; it gave me more goals to shoot for. I was like, 'Okay, I'd like to do that again someday.' "

Taylor loves working with Nathan on her albums as he's super talented and she enjoys creating music that her fans will love. They recorded most of the songs for her third album, *Speak Now*, in his basement. Nathan revealed to *Sound on Sound*: "Taylor and I made the demos for the first album at my then studio, with me playing all the instruments. When I was given the job of actually producing three songs, and then almost the whole of the record, we took these demos into a few professional studios and tracked them there with a small band.

"For the next album, *Fearless*, we went into a professional studio without me having heard the songs before. Taylor played me her songs right there and then, while the band was waiting, and I charted them and we cut the tracks live in the studio, with me playing guitar, plus a bassist and a drummer, and Taylor singing live. We added the other instruments as overdubs.

"With *Speak Now* [her third album], we deliberately went back to our initial way of working together. We had an unlimited budget, and could have gone and recorded the whole album in the Bahamas, used any studio we liked and whatever musicians we wanted. But we decided to bring it back to the basics on purpose, because we wanted to keep it about the music and our chemistry."

He went on to explain why making the second album had been easier: "We were coming off the momentum of the first album, and we simply continued the artistic track that we were on. It sold like crazy and won all these Grammy Awards and we're very proud of it. After all that, we wanted to keep ourselves out of a place of failure, and not try to overcompensate for the pressure we were feeling for a follow-up to *Fearless*. That's why we stripped it down and made the demos first. Taylor came to my studio and I played all the instruments on the demos, and because I have a good vocal booth, her demo vocals ended up being the vocals you hear on the record. After finishing the demos, we went out to different studios, and tried different combinations of engineers and musicians to replace some of the elements of my demos, mostly the programed drums, and to do additional overdubs."

Taylor revealed to *Country Weekly*: "I would write songs, drive to his house, and we would build the track from the ground up, and at that point we would establish a vibe from what that song needed. We would pick and choose different musicians to come and play on those songs based on the vibe we wanted, the sounds we wanted, and what we felt they could bring. A lot of times we got a magical first-take vocal and we would keep it."

The last song Taylor wrote for *Speak Now* was "The Story Of Us" and as soon as they finished it, they danced around the studio to celebrate the end of another chapter. When it was sent to music critics to review, they were impressed—with *Rolling Stone* stating the album "is roughly twice as good as 2008's *Fearless*, which was roughly twice as good as her 2006 debut."

Taylor's fourth album, *Red*, produced by Nathan Chapman, delighted both critics and fans alike when it was released in 2012, selling 1,208 million copies in the first week alone—a feat no other album had managed since 2002. It was another album that people enjoyed analyzing to try and figure out who she was singing about in her songs.

In November 2012, Guy Raz from NPR Music told Taylor that he'd come to the conclusion that she'd dated a lot of jerks. Taylor laughed and then replied: "I've written all my songs on every single one of my records, and that's what's been fun about looking back. My first album is the diary of when I was fourteen, fifteen, sixteen . . . My second album, *Fearless*, was from sixteen to eighteen, and so on, and so on. So you have my life being recorded in journal entries from these two-year periods of my life since I was sixteen.

"I like to write about love and love lost because I feel like there are so many different subcategories of emotions that you can possibly delve into. I've never missed two people the same way—it's always different for me. I've never fallen in love with someone and had the same exact kind of feeling come over me. So I think that there are all these different mixtures of emotions that go into individual feelings that you feel for individual people. And, yeah, most of the time it doesn't work out.

"That's the thing with love: it's going to be wrong until it's right. So you experience these different shades of wrong, and you miss the good things about those people, and you regret not seeing the red flags for the bad things about those people, but it's all a learning process. And being twenty-two, you're kind of in a crash course with love and life and lessons and learning the hard way, and thankfully, I've been able to write about those emotions as they've affected me."

Guy Raz also asked her whether she saw her lyrics as a way of directly communicating with her fans. She replied: "The first thing that I think about when I'm writing my lyrics is directly communicating with the person the song is about. I think what I've learned recently is that it's not heartbreak that inspires my songs. It's not love that inspires my songs. It's individual people that come into my life. I've had relationships with people that were really substantial and meant a lot to me, but I couldn't write a song about that person for some reason. Then again, you'll meet someone that comes into your life for two weeks and you write an entire record about them. When I first started writing songs, I was always scared that my songs were too personal—like, if I put someone's name in a song, people won't relate to it as much. But what I saw happening was, if I let my fans into my life and my feelings and what I'm going through—my vulnerabilities, my fears, my insecurities—it turns out they have all those things, too, and it kind of connects us."

DID YOU KNOW?

"Love Story," the lead single from Taylor's *Fearless* album, is thought to be about singer Joe Jonas of the Jonas Brothers. In the press kit for the album Taylor admitted: "I was dating a guy who wasn't exactly the popular choice. His situation was a little complicated, but I didn't care. When I wrote the ending to this song, I felt like it was the ending every girl wants to go with her love story. It's the ending I want. You want a guy who doesn't care what anyone thinks, what anyone says."

Taylor and Joe had a messy breakup, with Taylor telling the press the reason they finished was because Joe had been seeing actress Camilla Belle for months. She told fans he'd dumped her in a phone call lasting twenty-seven seconds, and posted a funny video on her YouTube of herself with a Joe Jonas doll that came with a phone so he can "break up with other dolls."

SHELLBACK AND MAX MARTIN

Taylor has had the opportunity to work with some of her dream collaborators on her albums. These include the talented songwriters and producers Shellback and Max Martin. They really challenge Taylor whenever they work together, in order to get the best out of her.

Together they produced and cowrote "We Are Never Ever Getting Back Together," "I Knew You Were Trouble" and "22" from her *Red* album, and "Shake It Off," "Blank Space," "Style" and "Bad Blood" from her fifth album, *1989*.

Taylor really enjoys working with Shellback and Max Martin. When she was chatting to *Billboard* about writing "22" and the fact that twenty-two seems to be the ideal age, she said: "For me, being twenty-two has been my favorite year of my life. I like all the possibilities of how you're still learning, but you know enough. You still know nothing, but you know that you know nothing. You're old enough to start planning your life, but you're young enough to know there are so many unanswered questions. That brings about a carefree feeling that is sort of based on indecision and fear and at the same time letting loose. Being twenty-two has taught me so much."

She told journalist Phil Gallo: "I have always been so fascinated by how [producer] Max Martin can just land a chorus. He comes at you and hits you and it's a chorus—all caps, with exclamation points."

She also confessed that she'd decided to work with Max, Shellback, Ed Sheeran, Dan Wilson and Gary Lightbody rather than just work with Nathan Chapman because it got her out of her comfort zone. She explained: "I turned in twenty songs and I had this immediate sinking feeling, this can't be done, this can't be it. I think the reason I said that was because I made the record [*Red*] exactly the same way I made the last three. I knew I hadn't jumped out of my comfort zone, which at the time was writing alone and working with Nathan. "Red" the song was a real turning point for *Red* the album. When I wrote that song my mind started wandering to all the places we could go.

If I were to think outside the box enough, go in with different people, I could learn from and have what they do rub off on me as well as have what I do rub off on them."

Taylor had been thrilled to have the opportunity to work with Ed Sheeran because she'd fallen in love with his music, even though his album hadn't been released in America at that time. When she approached his people she found out that he'd been hoping they'd work together someday. They wrote their track, "Everything Has Changed," while sitting on a trampoline in Taylor's garden. The pair had only one guitar between them, so they had to take it in turns to play. Afterwards, they ate apple pie that Taylor and her friends had made.

Taylor's fifth album, *1989*, was released on October 27, 2014, and was her "first documented, official pop album." It sold more copies in the US than any other album that year and was a huge hit worldwide. She chose to give the album the title "1989" (the year of her birth) because she'd listened to music from that year during the songwriting process and had found it inspiring.

Prior to the release, she told *Rolling Stone* magazine: "I used to talk about Max Martin like he was this sorcerer who lived in a castle on a hill. And then one time Scott [Borchetta] said to me, 'You know, you can work with him if you want to.' I was like, *What?!*

"[The 1980s] was a very experimental time in pop music. People realized songs didn't have to be this standard drums-guitar-bass-whatever. We can make a song with synths and a drum pad. We can do group vocals the entire song. We can do

DID YOU KNOW?

Taylor was in the studio with Shellback and Max when a situation happened that resulted in "We Are Never Ever Getting Back Together" being written. She revealed to MTV: "We were in the middle of writing a different song and this guy walked into this studio randomly and he's like, 'I'm friends with your ex-boyfriend. I heard you guys are getting back together.' But as soon as he left, I just started going on this rant. So Max said, 'You seem really passionate about it. You should write a song about it.' We just created this song in, like, thirty minutes. It came from a very real place and it came from a very spontaneous situation."

Taylor was so pleased with the finished song because she knew her ex would find it irritating every time he heard it on the radio. The video would also irritate him as she pokes fun at him throughout. Swifties think it's clearly about Jake Gyllenhaal because the actor playing her ex looks very similar to him, she waves around the scarf that she wore when they were dating, and her band are dressed as animals, which they believe is a shout-out to the human rabbit in Gyllenhaal's movie, *Donnie Darko* (2001).

so many different things. And I think what you saw happening with music was also happening in our culture, where people were just wearing whatever crazy colors they wanted to, because why not? There just seemed to be this energy about endless opportunities, endless possibilities, endless ways you could live your life. And so with this record, I thought, *There are no rules to this. I don't need to use the same musicians I've used, or the same band, or the same producers, or the same formula. I can make whatever record I want.*"

DID YOU KNOW?

Taylor's friend, musician-songwriter Jack Antonoff, cowrote and coproduced two tracks for *1989*. They both love the 1980s band Fine Young Cannibals' song, "She Drives Me Crazy. "

CHAPTER 2

HOME IS WHERE THE MUSIC IS

For Taylor, home will always be the US. Her first home was an eleven-acre Christmas tree farm in Cumru Township, Berks County, Pennsylvania. Originally owned by Taylor's grandfather, it was a wonderful place to live.

Taylor found living on the farm magical and had great fun exploring nature with her brother Austin.

Andrea and Scott would regularly take Taylor and Austin to the local cinema and this is something the whole family enjoyed. As they drove home, Taylor would sing the songs she'd heard in the movie that day, word for word. This was truly remarkable as most people need to hear a song a few times in order to recall it, but not Taylor, and she was only a young child.

Her earliest performances took place in the family lounge as a three-year-old. She enjoying singing "Unchained Melody" by the Righteous Brothers and receiving a round of applause at the end. She would also sing in school and in church.

Taylor's preschool was the Alvernia Montessori School in Reading, Pennsylvania. It was run by nuns, and the school's head teacher, Sister Anne Marie Coll, never forgot Taylor. Sister Anne told her local paper, the *Reading Eagle*: "She was kind of shy, but not too shy, and she always liked to sing. When she was in grade school, she came back and played guitar for the children. When she would put her mind to something, she was very intent."

DID YOU KNOW?

In 2009, Taylor donated $250,000 to the schools she attended as a child, with Alvernia Montessori School receiving $5,000.

Despite being shy at times, Taylor enjoyed standing out and being noticed. When she was five she posed so much during a family photo shoot that the photographer told her mom she had the potential to become a child model in Los Angeles. This wasn't something that appealed to Andrea or Scott at all—they still thought at this point that their daughter would end up working in finance.

Taylor used to love listening to all kinds of music when she was growing up. She especially liked country music, but her mom preferred English rock band Def Leppard to country any day. Taylor told the *Guardian*: "LeAnn Rimes was my first impression of country music. I got her first album when I was six. I just really loved how she could be making music and having a career at such a young age."

DID YOU KNOW?

When Taylor was eight she went to see country singer LeAnn Rimes perform in concert in Atlantic City. She loved every second, especially when LeAnn reached out and touched her hand. Afterward, Taylor loved telling all her friends what had happened.

Andrea and Scott bought Taylor her first guitar for Christmas, an electric, when she was eight years old. She didn't find it easy to play and for many years it sat gathering dust. One day, a man came to her home to fix the family computer and he spotted the guitar. He asked Taylor about it and offered to teach her a few chords. After a few minutes she was hooked and started practicing as much as she could. Her mom admitted to *Glamour* that "she was driven beyond anything I had ever witnessed" and that her fingers cracked from playing so much.

Taylor confided in a teacher that she wanted to play an acoustic twelve-string but they told her that it was too complex. She confessed to *Teen Vogue* magazine: "I actually learned on a twelve-string, purely because some guy told me that I'd never be able to play it, that my fingers were too small. Anytime someone tells me that I can't do something, I want to do it more."

By the time Taylor was eleven, she was spending her weekends singing karaoke—songs by Shania Twain, Dixie Chicks and Faith Hill were her speciality. When she wasn't at school, she'd spend hours listening to songs by country legends Dolly Parton and Patsy Cline. Taylor found country artists to be such good storytellers, but she also liked pop artists like Natasha Bedingfield, Hanson and the Spice Girls. She would try to copy the dance moves of Backstreet Boys and Britney Spears from their music videos but she was never very good at it; dancing just wasn't her thing.

In April 2009 Taylor told *Time* magazine that her biggest musical influence growing up was Shania Twain. She said: "She came out, and she was just so strong and so independent and wrote all her own songs. That meant so much to me, even as a ten-year-old. Just knowing that the stories she was telling in those songs—those were her stories."

Taylor decided to follow in Shania's footsteps and starting writing songs of her own in her bedroom. She also experimented with poetry, telling the *Washington Post* in February 2008: "It started with poetry, trying to figure out the perfect combination of words, with the perfect amount of syllables and the perfect rhyme to make it completely pop off the page. I started when I was ten and won this national poetry contest."

Taylor's poem was titled "The Monster in My Closet." She had purposefully chosen a poem that she thought the judges would love, the most gimmicky out of all the ones she'd written. Despite her young age, she found writing poems that rhymed pretty easy, whereas many of her classmates struggled if their English teacher ever asked them to write a poem for homework.

In addition to listening to music, writing songs and composing poetry in her spare time, Taylor would devour books. She really enjoyed *The Giving Tree* by Shel Silverstein and the Amelia Bedelia series by Peggy Parish. Every night before she went sleep she would get her mom to read her a bedtime story and always wanted new ones, which drove Andrea a little crazy at times.

Taylor confessed to the *Daily Mail*: "When I first started writing songs I was pretty lonely. I was about twelve and at school in Pennsylvania. I wasn't popular and didn't have many friends, and never knew where to sit at lunch. But songwriting became a release. I'd think, 'Okay, three more classes to go and then I can write about this,' so it became a reward. I didn't know how to articulate my feelings, but I'd strum my guitar and the words would come out. It allowed me to understand better the way I felt and get through it."

DID YOU KNOW?

When Taylor was thirteen or fourteen years old she spent her summer holiday writing a novel—and it was 350 pages long. It was based on her life and her friends, but she's never made it public. Many Swifties think it could be quite dark in parts because she's mentioned in the past that she used to dream up stories for the squirrels and birds her cats used to kill when she lived on the farm.

Taylor loved growing up in the countryside, riding on a tractor with her dad, playing outside with her brother, Austin, building forts out of haystacks and helping her mom with simple tasks. Her hair would be tangled and her clothes filthy, but it didn't matter when she was having fun.

One day she was supposed to check the Christmas trees on the farm for praying mantises but she forgot and it caused all sorts of trouble in the neighborhood. She revealed to Jay Leno on *The Tonight Show*: "There were hundreds of thousands of them . . . and they had little kids and they couldn't kill them because that'd be a bad Christmas."

Taylor used scold herself off rather than wait for her parents to do it—no doubt she gave herself a hard time that particular day. She admitted to journalist Lina Das from the *Daily Mail* in October 2012: "When I was naughty as a kid, I used to send myself to my own room. My mom says that she was afraid to punish me sometimes because I was so hard on myself when I did something wrong. I haven't changed much since then. I live half my life in the present and half of it as an eighty-year-old grandmother. My grandkids will be able to read about what I got up to as a twenty-two-year-old, so I want to make sure that they're reading things that are good. I know that's forward planning to a crazy degree, but I want them to be proud of me."

When she was ten, Taylor decided that she wanted to perform onstage and so she joined her local children's theater: Berks County Youth Theater Academy. After seeing the group's performance of *Charlie and the Chocolate Factory* she had made up her mind: acting was for her since it would allow her to sing onstage to an audience. She had already played a character called Freddy Fast Talk in another production and had acted in school, so she had some experience.

Taylor was determined to act and was willing to play any kind of role, male or female. She explained to E! how she got the part of Freddy: "I was like, 'I will dress up like a guy, I want to sing that song.' I had, like, a mustache, and we drew on eyebrows and put all my hair up in this hat, and I dressed like a guy and sang solo."

Taylor auditioned for the group's next production, the musical *Annie*. She did really well and they welcomed her with open arms. There were lots of ambitious young actors and actresses in the group and Taylor fit in well. She started out a bit self-conscious because she was taller than many of the other children, but this was actually a good thing as it allowed her to play adults easily. After having a small part in *Annie*, Taylor secured the lead in the next production, Maria in *The Sound of Music*. This was the perfect role for her and she really excelled as she sang classics like "My Favorite Things," "Do-Re-Mi" and "Edelweiss." The organizers who ran the group decided to let her perform every show, rather than allow her understudy to take over for half the week—she was simply too good.

When they decided to put on the musical *Grease* it was clear that there was only one girl to play Sandy—it was a role made for Taylor. As she sang songs like "Summer Nights," "Hopelessly Devoted To You" and "You're The One That I Want" in rehearsals, her vocals had a country twang to them. Taylor really wasn't that surprised as she loved listening to country music, but the person in charge of the theater group wasn't overjoyed and gave her vocal lessons in an attempt to take away her country twang.

DID YOU KNOW?

For the role of Sandy, Taylor had to learn how to walk in heels and so she had to take some lessons. She found it difficult at first but soon got the hang of it.

When she was onstage performing, Taylor realized that country music was her passion and the direction she should go in. However, the theater group's director thought she had the potential to be a huge Broadway star and invited her to join three other girls in a group called "Broadway in Training." Together they traveled to New York to audition for roles when they weren't in school. Competition was fierce and it was hard to stand out when there was a long line of girls auditioning for the same part.

Taylor managed to secure a part in a movie and attended rehearsals, but then it was canceled, which was disappointing. Together with the three other girls in the group she was given the opportunity to perform at Disney World one day, which was an amazing experience. She started performing in a sketch comedy group that performed weekly, which was something she really enjoyed, but after a while the group disbanded.

She continued to perform in productions with Berks County Youth Theater Academy, but after their production of *Bye Bye Birdie*, she felt it was time to move on. Her passion was singing, not acting. She actually looked forward to the after-show parties more than the shows themselves because she could use the karaoke machine and sing her favorite songs. If you search for "Taylor Swift Bye Bye Birdie" on YouTube you'll be able to see a short clip of her performance.

Taylor wanted to pursue her music, and her parents were behind her every step of the way. They believed she could be whatever she wanted to be. She admitted to the *Independent*: "When I was younger, probably six or seven, I used to follow my dad around and say, 'I'm gonna be stockbroker like you,' and I had no idea what a stockbroker was, of course! But as I grew up, my parents would always just say to me, 'You can do whatever you wanna do in life—as long as you work hard to get there. You have to work hard for every single baby step that you get that is closer to what you want. And we will support that until you change your mind and want something else. And when you want something else, we will be your cheerleaders in that too.' "

Taylor started taking part in karaoke competitions in bars in her local area. It wasn't ideal, but with Andrea and Scott acting as her chaperones she was always safe. Every week she would perform at country singer Pat Garrett's Roadhouse bar, eager to entertain and bring her music to a bigger audience.

She revealed to CMT News: "I started out singing karaoke in his roadhouse—his little bar—when I was ten years old. He'll vouch that I was in there every single week saying, 'I'm just going to come back if you don't let me win one.' I was kind of like an annoying fly around that place. I just would not leave them alone. What they would do is have these karaoke contests. And if you won, you got to open for, like, Charlie Daniels or George Jones. I would go until I would win."

Taylor would sing and play guitar for anyone who would listen, performing in cafés, coffee shops and community centers. When she opened for country star Charlie Daniels, she realized that she should be trying to sing for bigger audiences more often—the buzz it gave her was incredible and it was a better way of promoting herself.

She decided to target local sports teams who needed singers to perform the National Anthem at their games, as she explained to *Rolling Stone*: "I figured out that if you could sing that one song, you could get in front of 20,000 people without even having a record deal."

Taylor really enjoyed performing at baseball games for the Reading Phillies, at the US Open and a basketball game for the Philadelphia 76ers, among others. She kind of fell into it by accident—on August 8, 2000, she had been at the FirstEngery Stadium in Reading, PA to perform a few songs from *Grease* with the rest of her drama group when the singer booked to perform the National Anthem didn't turn up. Taylor might have only been ten at the time, but she was eager to seize the opportunity and to show everyone watching the game how well she could sing.

The team's general manager, Scott Hunsicker, was the man who handed Taylor the microphone that day. He confessed to the *Reading Eagle* that she was nervous at first as she quickly practiced the words with mom Andrea: "But when she stepped to the mic, it was as if she had done it a thousand times. There's just something inside her like an athlete would have, or in this case, a world-class performer would have. It's just like, boom [snapping his fingers], the switch flips, there's a pull, the game slows down."

For Taylor her performance at the Philadelphia 76ers game in the spring of 2002 was a huge deal and she decided to look as patriotic as possible by wearing a top with an American flag design. You can watch her performance for yourself if you search for "Philadelphia 76ers Taylor Swift" on YouTube. She might have been nervous, but rapper Jay-Z was sitting in the audience and thought she did great, giving her a high-five as she passed him.

Her next big performance was at the World Series game between the Philadelphia Phillies and the Tampa Bay Rays in 2008. By this point, she'd sung the National Anthem hundreds of times, but naturally, she was still nervous. She confessed to CMT News back then: "The National Anthem is not as challenging range-wise because I've been doing it for so long. The challenge for me is the utter silence that comes over 40,000 people in a baseball stadium and you're the only one singing it . . . it's a really surreal moment for me."

In a separate interview with *Elle Girl* magazine, she admitted: "It was a little scary at first. Every time you play another show it gets better and better."

DID YOU KNOW?

One day, Taylor's local paper mentioned one of her National Anthem performances, but instead of it making her really happy, she felt a bit nervous because she knew she'd be teased the next day in school. So many students were jealous of her talent.

Taylor's vocal coach/manager from the theater school, Kirk Cremer, encouraged her to record a demo with his brother Ronnie, who owned a recording studio. Taylor really enjoyed choosing which songs to sing and being in the recording studio itself. She decided to perform the country classics "One Way Ticket" by LeAnn Rimes, "Here You Come Again" by Dolly Parton, "There's Your Trouble" by Dixie Chicks and "Hopelessly Devoted To You" from *Grease*.

By this point, Taylor and her family were no longer living at the Christmas tree farm; instead, they were living in a six-bedroom house on Grandview Boulevard in Reading, Pennsylvania. The property was large and Taylor's bedroom was in the attic. It was a luxurious house and some of her friends may have been a little envious of the fact that she had an indoor swimming pool, but Taylor never lorded her family's wealth over anyone.

Every summer they headed to their holiday home in Stone Harbor, New Jersey, a place Taylor says was where most of her childhood memories were formed. They would spend lots of time by the water, swimming, jet-skiing and sailing. Her family love boats and when Taylor was growing up, they had a vintage Chris-Craft and Sea Rays powerboats. She and her brother Austin practically lived in lifejackets all summer.

Taylor confessed to Jonathan Van Meter from *Vogue*: "We lived on this basin where all this magical stuff would happen. One time a dolphin swam into our basin. We had this family of otters that would live on our dock at night. We'd turn the light on and you'd see them, you know, hanging out, just being otters. And then one summer, there was a shark that washed up on our dock. I ended up writing a novel that summer because I wouldn't go in the water. I locked myself in the den and wrote a book."

Taylor would sing karaoke at Henny's Seafood restaurant and put on shows at Coffee Talk café. She revealed to Robert Strauss from the *Inquirer*: "When I would run out of material, I'd just start making up songs on the spot.

"We used to all gather together on the dock when the boat parades would go by on July 4 and we'd shoot water balloons at them.

"I made a clubhouse in the room above my garage and made a filing system of members of the club. Everyone had a profile that I would write on tiles I found. I painted the whole room different colors and used to spend all day in there just doing nothing but sitting in my little club. Because it was mine.

"We lived across from the bird sanctuary and I had a pair of binoculars, and some days I'd just stare at the window, looking for birds. Or the boy who lived next door to me, whom I swore I would marry someday. One summer when I was eleven, I wrote a novel. I was allowed to be kind of weird and quirky and imaginative as a kid, and that was my favorite part of living at the Shore."

DID YOU KNOW?

Taylor's parents sold their holiday home when she was fourteen, but she still made the occasional trip back. While touring with Brad Paisley, she took her band with her and they had a great day checking out some of Taylor's favorite places. She used to love going to Springer's ice cream shop and having cookie-dough ice cream, and her favorite place to eat was the Italian Garden restaurant.

One of the places in the world that means the most to Taylor is Nashville, Tennessee. She first visited the city when she was eleven and moved there with her family when she was fourteen.

Taylor first decided that she wanted to live in Nashville after she'd watched a documentary on one of her musical heroes,

Faith Hill. Faith had moved to Nashville from Mississippi in order to give her music career a kick-start. Nashville was the home of country music and if Taylor wanted to become a country singer, she figured it was the place to be.

She began pestering her mom and dad, asking repeatedly, "Hey, Mom and Dad, can we move to Nashville?" They were settled in Pennsylvania, so didn't immediately say yes, but as a compromise Andrea said she would take her there during spring break. Andrea revealed to *Women's Health* magazine in November 2008: "It was never about 'I want to be famous.' Taylor never uttered those words. It was about moving to a place where she could write, with people she could learn from."

Nashville was over 650 miles away, so it was a big commitment on Andrea's part to drive Taylor and her brother Austin there. Taylor's big plan was to deliver her demo CDs to all the country record labels she could find, and Andrea was keen to help her as much as she could, but she wouldn't go inside with her—Taylor had to do that on her own.

DID YOU KNOW?

The front of Taylor's demo CD has a photo of her face and "Call me" on it. On the back is her telephone number and email address. As she delivered each CD to the person at reception, she would say, "Call me!"

Taylor had been hoping that giving out demo CDs in this way would work, but alas, it didn't. She waited weeks for someone to pick up the phone and call or send her a message saying they wanted to hear more, but no one did. Eventually she received one call from a guy who wanted to offer some advice: her pitch had little chance of working because there were so many other people doing exactly the same. Taylor was still touched that he took the time out to call her. Now, she needed to think of a new plan.

In the meantime, she was still performing the National Anthem at sport events and one day, a man called Dan Dymtrow heard her sing and thought she had potential. He was the manager of pop superstar Britney Spears and wanted to find out more about her. Taylor's dad came up with the idea of putting together a home video that showed her personality and just how she was. Dan was impressed when he saw it and invited Taylor and her parents to his office. Taylor took along her guitar so she could perform and this led to him putting her forward for a photo shoot for *Vanity Fair* magazine. Although this was more of a modeling gig than anything else, the shoot was for a campaign called "Rising Stars." The idea was that they would showcase potential stars of the future while promoting clothing by Abercrombie & Fitch.

DID YOU KNOW?

Taylor had mixed emotions when it came to the *Vanity Fair* photo shoot because the bullying she'd experienced at school had made her self-conscious. She didn't think she was as cool as the other people who were taking part, but her new manager did.

The magazine came out in July 2004 and Taylor was so pleased to have been given a full page. To see herself in a big magazine felt incredible and she knew the short interview accompanying her photo could potentially lead to people checking out her music online.

In the interview she'd said: "After I sang the National Anthem at the US Open last year a top music manager signed me as his client. I love the sound of fiddles and mandolins ringing in my ears and I love the stories that you hear in country ballads. I sometimes write about teenage love, but I am presently a fourteen-year-old girl without a boyfriend. Sometimes I worry that I must be wearing some kind of guy repellent, but then I realize that I'm just discovering who I am as a person.

"Right now, music is the most important thing in my life, and I want to touch people with my songs."

Dan Dymtrow wanted to get Taylor's music heard and he managed to get one of her songs on a promotional album called *Chicks with Attitudes* that American cosmetics brand Maybelline was putting together. He also secured several meetings with record labels and it was through him that Taylor got her development deal with RCA Records.

She really needed to be based in Nashville, so her parents decided to make the move. Her dad could do his job from anywhere and both he and mom Andrea wanted to support their daughter as much as they could. Taylor admitted to *Blender* magazine: "My parents moved across the country so I could pursue a dream." Austin wanted to support his sister too and agreed to make Nashville his new home, even though leaving his friends behind was tough.Reflecting on this time, Taylor told *Self* magazine: "I knew I was the reason they were moving, but they tried to put no pressure on me. They were like, 'Well, we need a change of scenery anyway' and, 'I love how friendly people in Tennessee are.' "

Andrea explained to *Entertainment Weekly*: "I never wanted to make that move about her 'making it.' Because what a horrible thing if it hadn't happened, for her to carry that kind of guilt or pressure around. And we moved far enough outside Nashville to where she didn't have to be going to school with producers' kids and label presidents' kids and be reminded constantly that she was struggling to make it. We've always told her that this is not about putting food on our table or making our dreams come true. There would always be an escape hatch into normal life if she decided this wasn't something she had to pursue. And of course that's like saying to her, 'If you want to stop breathing, that's cool.' "

When it came to choosing the perfect home in Nashville, Andrea worked fast and soon found a property on Old Hickory Lane that she liked. Scott was sold before he even stepped inside the house, telling the Sea Ray website: "We stopped at the dock on the way to check up on the house. I looked down the cove toward the lake, imagined my Sea Ray tied up there and said, 'I'll take it.' "

Once they moved in, Taylor and Austin started at the local high school, Hendersonville. The students welcomed them both with open arms and Taylor immediately felt relieved. She told *The New Yorker*: "Everybody was so nice to me . . . they're all, like, 'We heard you're a singer. We have a talent show next week—do you want to enter?' "

DID YOU KNOW?

Taylor wrote her song, "A Place In This World," for her debut album based on those early days in Nashville. Although happy to finally be there, she felt like a small fish in a very big pond. She explained to Great American Country TV: "I was just sort of looking around at all these big buildings and these important people, wondering how I was going to fit in."

Taylor will be forever grateful that her parents were willing to move to Nashville. When she won the Horizon Award at the 2007 Country Music Awards, on November 7, she thanked them in her speech. She said: "I can't even believe that this is real . . . I want to thank God, and my family for moving to Nashville so I could do this. I want to thank Country Radio; I will never forget the chance you took on me. Brad Paisley, thank you for letting me tour with you." She also thanked Scott Borchetta and the whole team at Big Machine Records before thanking her fans for changing her life.

The next month, she was shocked to discover that she'd been nominated in the Best New Artist category at the Grammy Awards. It sure was a great way to end 2007.

Over the years Taylor has become an ambassador for Nashville, and she confessed to the Associated Press in October 2013 that she encouraged Ed Sheeran to move to the city. She said: "Ed loves Nashville. You know, so many people live here now. It's really exciting, because nobody who comes here doesn't like it, and it just makes me proud to live here and it makes me proud to make music here and I love it. I just love it becoming such an exciting place to live."

Taylor bought her first property in Nashville back in the autumn of 2009. She'd loved the fact that the penthouse apartment had amazing views of the city when she'd been to view the property for the first time but hated the décor—so had great fun completely changing everything in sight. She added a fish pond to the middle of her apartment, with a human-sized bird cage hanging down, and mismatched her furniture. She wanted her home to reflect her personality and wasn't afraid to create something truly unique.

Although she missed her family, she wasn't far away and still visited them most days. She revealed to TV host Chelsea Handler: "Living alone, you can do so many fantastic things. You can walk around and have conversations with yourself and, like, sing your thoughts. I think I'm the only one who does that!"

As soon as she became a homeowner she felt more mature, telling TV host Lesley Stahl: "I walked into this apartment after I bought it and thought, *Oh man, this is real now*. We're all getting older, and soon my parents are going to be older, and then I have to think about grown-up things."

In October 2013, Nashville Songwriters Association International announced that Taylor had won their Songwriter/Artist of the Year award for the sixth year running. No other artist had ever won the award six times, and she was also the youngest ever winner. What a wonderful achievement!

DID YOU KNOW?

Taylor wrote her track, "Never Grow Up," from her third studio album, *Speak Now*, after she bought her apartment. She admits: " 'Never Grow Up' is a song about the fact that I don't quite know how I feel about growing up. It's tricky. Growing up happens without you knowing it. Growing up is such a crazy concept because a lot of times when you were younger, you wish you were older. I look out into a crowd every night and I see a lot of girls that are my age and going through exactly the same things as I'm going through. Every once in a while I look down and I see a little girl who is seven or eight, and I wish I could tell her all of this. There she is becoming who she is going to be and forming her thoughts and dreams and opinions. I wrote this song for those little girls."

Taylor decided to use this opportunity to announce that she was opening her own school at the Country Music Hall of Fame and Museum in Nashville. She wanted the Taylor Swift Education Center to help musically talented children to learn and grow, and was putting $4 million of her own money into the project. Taylor told journalists: "In school, I was taught a certain amount about music, a certain amount about theater, and that interest sparked something in me. It made me look elsewhere to learn much more about it.

"I think, for me, it's just going to be so interesting to see Nashville continue to be this hub for music, and this hub for music education."

Another city that means a lot to Taylor is New York. She bought a penthouse apartment there in early 2014 and wrote her song, "Welcome To New York," based on the excitement she felt. She revealed to *Rolling Stone*: "I was so intimidated by this city for so long. It's so big, with so many people. I thought I would never be able to make it here, because I wasn't something enough—bold enough, brave enough—to take on this huge city in all of its blaring honesty. And then at a certain point I just thought, *I'm ready*."

DID YOU KNOW?

Taylor's New York apartment was once owned by the *Lord of the Rings* director Peter Jackson.

When interviewed by Alan Light from *Billboard*, he commented that many people forget that Taylor grew up in Pennsylvania, just a few hours away from New York. She replied: "Oh yeah—people have no idea! I summered at the Jersey Shore every year. When I first discovered that I was in love with performing, I wanted to be in theater. So growing up, New York City was where I would come for auditions. I was ten, but I was as tall as a sixteen-year-old, and then you'd have a twenty-two-year-old who could play ten, and they'd get the role. Then I started taking voice lessons in the city, so my mom and I would drive two hours and have these adventures.

"I went to a Knicks game a few weeks ago, and people were like, 'Oh, it's your first Knicks game!' I actually have a photo of my first Knicks game. I was twelve years old and I was in a halftime talent competition, but I didn't win because the kid who won sang 'New York, New York,' and I was like, 'Here's a song I wrote about a boy in my class . . .' "

DID YOU KNOW?

Taylor decided to donate all the proceeds from her song "Welcome To New York," which amounted to $50,000, to New York's Department of Education to help public schools in her new city.

Taylor is really happy living in New York, confessing to journalist Josh Eells from *Rolling Stone:* "I really like my life right now. I have friends around me all the time. I've started painting more. I've been working out a lot. I've started to really take pride in being strong. I love the album I made. I love that I moved to New York. So in terms of being happy, I've never been closer to that."

Taylor's apartment has four guest bedrooms, which means she's always got plenty of space if her friends want to stay over. Supermodel Karlie Kloss is one such friend, and also *Girls* creator and star Lena Dunham. Taylor actually became friends with Lena after contacting her on Twitter. Lena's reply to Tay's message was: "I am so excited about the prospect of being friends with you that I added the adjective best in front of it.

"The idea that you like my show is so thrilling, and I can't wait to lavish you with praise in person."

Throughout the years Taylor has visited so many different cities in the US. She loves having the opportunity to meet fans and tries to give back whenever she can. While on her Fearless Tour in 2008 she donated $100,000 to the Red Cross in Cedar Rapids, Iowa, after they suffered a terrible flood.

DID YOU KNOW?

Taylor wrote "Enchanted" for her *Speak Now* album in a hotel room after meeting a guy in New York. She explained to Chris Willman from Yahoo Music what happened: "I had talked to him on email or something before, but I had never met him. And meeting him, it was this overwhelming feeling of, *I really hope that you're not in love with somebody.* And the whole entire way home, I remember the glittery New York City buildings passing by, and then just sitting there, thinking, am I ever going to talk to this person again? Using the word 'wonderstruck' was done on purpose because that's a word that person used one time in an email. And I don't think I've ever heard anybody use that term before, so I purposely wrote it in the song, so he would know."

Taylor never revealed the name of the guy in question but it's widely believed that she was singing about the electronica artist Adam Young. He wrote an open letter to her on his website. In it he says: "Everything about you is lovely. You're an immensely charming girl with a beautiful heart and more grace and elegance than I know how to describe. You are a true princess from a dreamy fairytale, and above all I just want you to know I was enchanted to meet you, too."

Adam went on to record a song about Taylor. To listen to it, search for "Owl City—Enchanted by Taylor Swift" on YouTube.

She told *People* magazine at the time: "The people in this town have been through so much loss this year, and my heart goes out to them. They've stood by me; they gave me a sold-out show. You've got to pay it forward in life—that's all I did in Cedar Rapids."

Over the years, Taylor has done so much for charities. She gave her merchandise sales from the CMA Music Festival in 2008 to the Nashville Red Cross and gave the pink pickup truck her record company gave her when she turned eighteen to a youth camp for sick children. She's also helped individuals: in 2015 she donated $50,000 to a young girl who had to miss one of her *1989* shows as she was in hospital being treated for leukaemia. Taylor wrote on the girl's GoFundMe page: "To the beautiful and brave Naomi, I'm sorry you have to miss it, but there will always be more concerts. Let's focus on getting you feeling better. I'm sending the biggest hugs to you and your family."

Before Taylor did her own tours, she was a supporting act for a number of big country singers. Her first tour was for the country band Rascal Flatts in 2008. They contacted her after their opening act dropped out and she had only two days to get ready—yikes! Taylor didn't mind that it was late notice—she was just grateful to have been given the opportunity.

After this tour, she was asked to support country legend George Strait for twenty dates. She learned a lot from him and when he namechecked her during his own set, she was on cloud nine, writing on her blog: "George Strait SAID MY NAME. We were watching George's show and all of a sudden he said, 'I'm very happy to have the talented Miss Taylor Swift out here with us.' YESSSS. It was pretty awesome, sort of a life-changing moment."

After George Strait came country rocker Brad Paisley. He told *Blender* magazine at the time: "I was looking at a lot of artists to come out on tour with us, but as soon as I downloaded her album, I knew we had to have her. I was floored by the songwriting. I love the fact that she doesn't pretend to be thirty years old in her songs. She has a very genuine voice."

DID YOU KNOW?

It was during the tour with Brad Paisley that Taylor became good friends with Kellie Pickler, a former contestant of the talent show *American Idol*, who was also supporting him. As they traveled around the US, the pair got to know each other really well and Taylor would offer Kellie love advice. The two of them would cause mischief too; even when Brad was onstage, he wasn't safe. One night he was performing his track "Ticks" when Taylor and Kellie came onto the stage dressed as ticks and his other supporting act, Jack Ingram, was dressed as an exterminator.

Taylor later wrote on her blog: "I was laughing so hard I could barely breathe. Then I was lying there on the stage playing dead and I looked up at Brad, and he looked down at me and said, 'Nice work.' Guess he was a little bit 'bugged.' "

When Taylor supported Kenny Chesney she liked the laid-back atmosphere and the way he treated the people around him. During the tour, she told *USA Today*: "Kenny is up at the crack of dawn, walking around the venue, getting to know everyone, from the sound-check guys to the fans."

Taylor loved supporting these country greats, but nothing compared to her very first tour, which kicked off in Evansville, Indiana, on April 23, 2009. Her supporting acts were Kellie Pickler, country group Gloriana and, for the UK dates, Justin Bieber. All in all, she played 112 dates around the world.

Taylor confessed to the *Victoria Advocate*: "I never wanted to go into an arena and have to downsize it so there were only 5,000 or 4,000 people there, so we waited a long time to make sure the headlining tour was everything I wanted a headlining tour to be."

But she needn't have worried about the demand for tickets—her whole tour sold out within a matter of minutes. She sold 40,000 tickets for her Madison Square Garden concert in less than a minute and her Staples Center concert sold out within two minutes. Fans were desperate to see her perform live and Taylor couldn't wait to put on the best show possible.

For years she'd been dreaming own headline tour, and supporting other artists on tour had given her plenty of inspiration. Back in January, when she first announced that she'd be touring, she told the press: "Headlining my own tour is a dream come true. This way, I can play more music every night than I ever have before. Having written my own songs, they are all stories in my head, and my goal for this tour is to bring those stories to life. My favorite thing when I go to a concert is having lots of changing things to look at, so I've been working really hard to make this show as multi-dimensional as possible.

I want to be sure that everyone has the opportunity to come see my show, so we have affordable tickets available for every date we do this year."

Taylor wanted her shows to be extra special, both onstage and backstage. A few days before the first show, she wrote in her blog: "I'm laying on a comfortable, beautiful couch in the backstage club house/living room/'T-party' room. It's a room I've always wanted to have on other tours. It looks nothing like backstage. It looks like your living room. The walls are covered in magenta/maroon/gold/purple draped fabric, and the floors are carpeted with oriental rugs on top. There are lanterns hanging from the ceiling and candles everywhere. In the middle of everything is a column with pictures of my band and me all over it. Pictures that remind me of home. Pictures with Kellie, Abigail, Selena [Gomez], my dad, my brother, the trip my band and crew and I took to Hawaii this summer . . . My dancers, my crew . . . Everyone's in a picture. That's just my favorite part of the room. The boys like the Ping-Pong table, foosball table, and the big screen TV entertainment center. So I'm in heaven right now, sitting on the couch, waiting for everyone to get here to rehearse."

Even planning her shows was fun for Taylor. Previously she'd shared: "I'm in heaven right now. Constantly having meetings with the video crew and the lighting guys and the carpenters and the band and running through things over and over and over again."

For Taylor, her first night in Evansville was unforgettable and because of this she'll always have a soft spot for the city and the stadium she performed in that night. Before she went onstage she enjoyed a huddle with her band, dancers and crew in the T-party room. She said: "I just want to say that I didn't have a senior class, I didn't have a sorority. You guys are my senior class, and you guys are my sorority, and you guys are my brothers and my sisters, and you guys are the people who are helping me become the person I'm going to be, and I just want to thank you for that, and I could not love you more. We are going to go out there onstage and be fearless."

To hear thousands of fans cheering her name and singing along to her songs felt incredible. Taylor was living her dream and every night she performed was special for different reasons. The fans she got to meet afterwards in the T-party room were so lovely and she felt truly blessed.

DID YOU KNOW?

Taylor is a perfectionist and is always striving to do things better. After the first show she had some ideas as to how they could improve the lighting before the next show. Her team was happy to make the changes she requested because they knew how much it mattered to her.

Shortly before her Australia tour dates, Taylor attended the 52nd Grammys at the Staples Center in Los Angeles. It was to be a wonderful night for Taylor as not only did she have the opportunity to perform alongside Stevie Nicks and Butch Walker but she also picked up four awards. During her acceptance speech for her first award—the Best Female Vocal Performance award for "White Horse"—she told everyone watching: "This is my first Grammy, you guys! This is a Grammy!"

Later, in her acceptance speech for Album of the Year, she shared: "All of us, when we're eighty years old and we are telling the same stories over and over again to our grandkids, and they're so annoyed with us, this is the story we're going to be telling over and over again—in 2010, we got to win Album of the Year at the Grammys."

Taylor had to jump straight back into touring, and once the tour finished in the summer, she also had to promote her next album, *Speak Now*.

Taylor's second tour was called the Speak Now World Tour and there were 110 dates in seventeen countries. It kicked off on February 9, 2011 in Singapore.

DID YOU KNOW?

During her show at the Staples Center, Los Angeles, Taylor performed her track, "White Horse," with country singer John Mayer. They ended up dating briefly and their relationship inspired the track, "Dear John," from her third album, *Speak Now*. While chatting to *People* magazine about the song, Taylor explained: "A lot of times when people's relationships end, they write an email to that person and say everything that they wish they would have said. A lot of times they don't push 'send.' That was a tough one to write and I guess putting it on the album was pushing 'send.' "

But John Mayer wasn't at all impressed when he heard the song, telling *Entertainment Weekly*: "It made me feel terrible—because I didn't deserve it. I'm pretty good at taking accountability now, and I never did anything to deserve that. It was a really lousy thing to do."

Taylor was just as passionate about this tour as she had been about her Fearless Tour and she wanted to put into practice everything she had learned the first time around to make it even bigger and better. She said in the press announcement: "I'm so excited to go back out on tour again in 2011! The FEARLESS Tour was so much fun and even more unforgettable than I ever imagined, and I can't wait to get back out and play my new music from *Speak Now*! The fans have been so amazing, and I'm thrilled to play in new cities around the world and meet even more of my fans in 2011!"

Indeed Taylor put on such an action-packed show that she was exhausted every evening by the time she collapsed into her seat on the tour bus. She confessed to TV host Katie Couric: "Going through these performances, it's like an athletic marathon. When I'm underneath the stage and then it pops me up like a toaster, and then I'm like, six feet in the air, and I'm like, *Made it through that . . . did the banjo song . . . okay . . . onto this next blocking . . . change clothes . . . flying above the crowd—awesome . . .* "

DID YOU KNOW?

Taylor ended 2011 on a high, winning *Billboard's* Woman of the Year award, their youngest ever winner. She was chosen for both her business and personal achievements. In 2011 alone she'd given away more than $1 million to charities across the US and beyond.

Taylor wanted her Speak Now World Tour to be very theatrical, so she played close attention to the details—the scenery, the costumes and the props. She wanted to surprise her fans and so had special guests join her onstage. Originally, she hadn't set out to do this, but when she invited rapper Nicki Minaj to join her onstage at her show at the Staples Center in Los Angeles, it all snowballed. Taylor had simply enjoyed listening to Nicki's track, "Super Bass," and thought it would be fun to have her perform it, but soon other world-class singers were asking if they could be her special guests at different shows.

This led to Justin Bieber, Jason Mraz, Selena Gomez, James Taylor, Usher, T.I., Shawn Colvin, Jim Adkins of Jimmy Eat World, Ronnie Dunn, Tim McGraw, Kenny Chesney and Hayley Williams from Paramore all making special appearances at different shows.

DID YOU KNOW?

When Taylor found out that one of her fans had been involved in a serious car accident at the Columbia concert venue, she wanted to help. She made sure seven-year-old Grace could attend a later concert once she recovered, and met her backstage before the show. The girl's mother told *People* magazine: "Taylor greeted Grace by her name and immediately knelt down and hugged her. She told Grace she had a cold and asked Grace to sing extra loud to help her out."

Taylor's third tour, for *Red*, saw her once again performing around the world. This time she had eighty-six tour dates, running from March 13, 2013 to June 12, 2014. It was a much bigger production than her earlier tours and by the end of the

North American leg she was suffering with a bad cold. She didn't want to let any of her fans down so she battled through, asking them to excuse her whenever she needed to go offstage to blow her nose!

SWIFTIES' STORIES

CHAPTER 3

AMERICA

Taylor Swift plays more shows in the US and spends more time here than anywhere else. So Swifties in the US have more stories than Swifties from any other country in the world!

Allysa is twenty and from Memphis, Tennessee. Her three favorite Taylor Swift songs are "All Too Well," "Fearless" and "Long Live." She says: "I love Taylor for so many reasons but my favorite thing about her is how selfless she is. She connects with her fans on a personal level—she's always willing to go the extra mile for us, because she knows we have gone the extra mile for her. Also, one of my favorite quotes is, 'There are two ways you can go with pain. You can let it destroy you, or you can use it as fuel to drive you to dream bigger, work harder.'

"Being a Swiftie in the United States is so much fun. When I think about you guys in other countries I feel bad because she doesn't come and visit as often as you guys wish she would, and everyone deserves some T-Swift! She spends most of her time in New York or Los Angeles, but when she's 'home' in Nashville (which is only three hours from where I live), I love knowing she's not far away. (Although, it is very hard to just 'casually run into Taylor Swift.')

"I was so shocked when someone from Taylor Nation sent me a direct message on Twitter in September 2014, asking for more information about me and how long I'd been a Swiftie. The next day they called me but I missed the call because I was in class, but thankfully, they rang me back a few hours later and invited me to a special event in Nashville that Sunday. To say I was excited would be an understatement.

"The next day two days were the longest days of my life. When Sunday finally came, my mom and I packed up and drove to Nashville. We arrived around 1:00 p.m. so we went shopping and grabbed some lunch. I was too nervous to eat, think or breathe. At 4:00 p.m. we drove to the 'secret location.' There was a long line of people waiting by a tent and I got out and waited with them. I made friends in line (Rebecca and Morgan), talking about where we were from and our excitement for what was ahead. Around 5:00 p.m., we got to a lady with a clipboard, who asked for the secret password they had given us on the phone and took our IDs to make sure we were on the list. After that, we signed a confidentiality agreement and a media release form. We were told we were going to someone's house—that was it. We then had to hand over our phones, wallets and anything else we had. We were patted down by security and then got on a bus.

"Once all the buses were loaded, we left the parking lot. We pulled down a really nice street and I had noticed police officers were stopping traffic—for us. We were backing into a beautiful gated white house. I couldn't believe it. We were at Taylor's parents' house. While on the bus waiting to get off, one of her bodyguards told us that Taylor handpicked each one of us to be here tonight. I lost it. (That would be the first of many times I cried that night.)

"We got off the bus and walked over to a garage area and waited patiently for her bodyguards to escort us to the backyard. It was so beautiful. There was a huge pool with fountains pouring into it, the landscaping was perfect and, *oh, look! Food!* There was a large selection of food laid out (pizza, sushi, chicken nuggets, chips and dips, etc.). I grabbed a slice of pizza and the cutest Diet Coke bottle. I was so nervous, I only had about three bites of that pizza, but it was good. Some photographers came around and were taking professional and Polaroid pictures of everyone. Then everyone started gathering around the door. WE WERE ABOUT TO GO INSIDE TAYLOR'S HOUSE!

"When we walked in, it smelled like the most beautiful holiday you could ever imagine. The candles, the pictures, the furniture, it was so Taylor Swift. We walked down some stairs to the living room, which was filled with huge fluffy pillows. We all squished in together and waited for Taylor. THEN SHE WALKED IN. THERE WAS TAYLOR SWIFT. THE ACTUAL TAYLOR SWIFT I HAVE BEEN IN LOVE WITH SINCE 2006. SHE IS A QUEEN. She was SO beautiful and tall and perfect, and wearing stilettos and a jet-black romper with lace underneath.

"Someone yelled, 'It's Becky!' and she said, 'No, Becky's dead, let's have a moment of silence for Becky.' And then we actually had a moment of silence for Becky. Most die-hard Swifties know about the Becky meme that went viral on Tumblr, but if you don't, a blogger posted an old photo of Taylor wearing a tiara with the message, 'This is a picture of my friend Becky. She used to be a happy, popular girl until one night she snorted marijuana at a party. She died instantly. Please, don't do marijuana. It's the most dangerous drug out there. Please don't wind up like Becky.' Somebody replied, 'Pretty sure that's Taylor Swift,' to which the post replied with the now famous line: 'No, it's Becky.'

"After the moment of silence, Tay sat in her chair and told us we were sitting in her parents' living room and that her parents were sitting right behind us. She then told us she had been stalking us on Twitter, Instagram and Tumblr for the past six months. WHAT! That was such a cool/embarrassing/I-can't-believe-Taylor-knows-who-I-am moment.

"Taylor then told us she wanted to play her entire *1989* album for us. She made us promise that we wouldn't share anything about the album, songs, lyrics or tracks until October 27. Of course, we agreed. We listened to the first six songs on the album and they were so perfect, I was so in love with them. She then said we were going to take an intermission to go to the bathroom, and she was going to bring out some things that she baked for us. (I was super excited about this part. I would be eating something Taylor Swift made!)

"She brought out trays of cookies and chocolate Rice Krispies treats, chai tea cookies with cinnamon eggnog icing, and dark chocolate peppermint cookies, AKA heaven! They were so good. I was actually touching Taylor Swift while she was passing out cookies that she made. I then looked over and saw someone holding sweet little Olivia Benson [Taylor's cat]. I made my way over there and ate the cookie as fast as I could. I got to hold Olivia and it was the best thing ever. SHE IS ACTUALLY THE SOFTEST THING EVER.

"Taylor then came over and was talking to us about Olivia. While I was holding her, I felt like I was dreaming. She then took Olivia over to the couch and asked someone if they thought her tail was too short for her body. She said that when she took her to the vet, he said that her tail was bent at birth. She looked perfect to me. Oh, and did I mention Scott (AKA Taylor's dad) came over to me while I was holding Olivia and told me I couldn't take her home. It's like he knew I was a crazy cat lady. Anyways, I made my way back to an open spot on the floor and Taylor walked back to her chair and we listened to the second half of the album. It just kept getting better and better.

"During the last song, I got to hold Olivia again and was dancing along to the song with the cat, and Taylor kept looking at us and smiling (I had to try so hard not to cry happy tears). Then 'Shake It Off' came on. WE HAD A DANCE PARTY IN TAYLOR SWIFT'S LIVING ROOM! That was a lot of fun. The whole house started to shake and I had never had this much fun. After the dance party sadly ended, we were taken back outside to the pool area. Again, more food. It was time for individual pictures with Taylor. I was in Group 7, so I had a while before I got to go inside. Scott and Andrea brought their dogs outside and hung out with us. I joined the group around Andrea and she was telling the story of the time she had to bring Meredith [Taylor's other cat] on a commercial flight because Taylor was flying to Australia. Meredith and Olivia get to roam around and use the bathroom on Taylor's plane, so when Mere wasn't allowed out of the cat carrier on this flight, she was one angry kitty. She was meowing so much Andrea took her to the bathroom with her travel litter box and thought that would take care of the problem. It didn't. She ended up letting Mere out on the plane and when someone asked about the cat, she told them it was her grandkitty and that it was her daughter Taylor's cat. Taylor Swift. People were all of a sudden fangirling over Meredith.

"After that story, Scott came over and asked us if we were having fun (ARE YOU KIDDING? THIS IS THE BEST NIGHT OF MY ENTIRE LIFE. YOU ARE ACTUALLY MAKING MY DREAMS COME TRUE! I GUESS I DON'T HAVE A BUCKET LIST ANYMORE). Someone asked him if he was nervous during 'Shake If Off' when the whole house began to shake. He was like, 'YES, Taylor has never had this many friends over. This house was built in the 1920s, so we don't know what's under the living-room floor.' OKAY, TAYLOR'S DAD JUST CALLED US HER FRIENDS. EXCUSE ME WHILE I CRY. AGAIN. Group 6 had just gone in the house. So you know what that meant. GROUP 7 WAS NEXT. WHAT WAS I GOING TO SAY AND HOW WAS I GOING TO TAKE A PICTURE?

"When we went inside, we lined up and anxiously waited our turn. When it was my turn, I walked down the stairs to Taylor, standing there with her arms wide open. ARE YOU KIDDING ME RIGHT NOW? TAYLOR SWIFT THE GLOBAL SUPERSTAR WAS ACTUALLY FOCUSING ON ME AND WANTED TO GIVE ME A HUG! We hugged and she told me she loved my dress, that it was 'so Audrey Hepburn.' I was like, 'THANK YOU! I THOUGHT OF YOU WHEN I BOUGHT THIS.' She said I was so sweet for doing that. She then went on to tell me she loved my accent. Excuse me? I do not have an accent. I actually got sassy with Taylor Swift. She was all like, 'Do you think we all have cute northern accents? No.' I was at such a loss for words. For eight years I never thought this day would come. Everything I had ever wanted to say to Taylor was gone. So we just took a picture. I was really unsure of how I wanted to look in this picture because I wanted it to look real (partially because I didn't even believe it myself). She said we could sit at the piano and look like someone had just interrupted our jam session (BTW, THIS WAS THE VERY PIANO THAT SHE WROTE 'I KNEW YOU WERE TROUBLE' ON). And then she was like, or you could hold my Grammy or something (which was the Grammy for 'White Horse'), but then she was like, 'I KNOW. How about I sit on your lap?!' I was thinking to myself, like, IS TAYLOR ACTUALLY ASKING TO SIT ON MY LAP BECAUSE, WHAT? THAT IS NOT EVEN A QUESTION. So I sat in her chair and she was like, 'Sorry if I'm really heavy.' Like, are you kidding me? We then took our Polaroid picture on a camera from 1989. How cool! We gave each other one last hug, I told her I loved her and she said she loved me back and thanked me for coming.

The last thing you ever have to do is thank me for coming. Are you kidding? You just made my life!

"I was escorted out the front door and back to the garage, where we started. I was given a Taylor bag full of all her new merchandise, which included two calendars, three T-shirts, and a '*1989* Listening Session Nashville, TN' key chain. That was so special to me because only eighty-nine of us have that. When I got back on the bus, everyone was sharing their pictures. It was so fun. Although we were sad to be leaving, we couldn't wait to get our hands on our phones and FINALLY share the secret we had been keeping for days. I will never forget this day. I have never felt more loved in a room full of strangers. I will never be able to repay Taylor or her management team for making this day the special-est day of my life."

Nick is eighteen and from Detroit, Michigan. His favorite three songs are "Enchanted," "All Too Well" and "You Are In Love." He says: "I have almost every piece of Taylor Swift merchandise available, every album, every magazine and poster, and basically anything else you can think of! Every wall in my bedroom is covered in posters.

"I've been to all of Taylor's concerts in Detroit and always have floor seats so I have the best view. I love making a giant poster to take with me, getting dressed up, meeting all the other Swifties and just singing and dancing and having a blast with Taylor! She makes the concerts so enjoyable and she never fails to make me cry every time!

"I am one of the biggest Taylor Swift fans! I stay home from school whenever she is on TV just so I can watch it live. I record every appearance, too, so I can go back and re-watch them 100,000 times! I know everything there is to know about Taylor and I would love to meet her someday or even get noticed by her on social media! If she sent me something in the mail or liked one of my tweets I would just be the happiest person in the world! Even if that never happened, just her being herself and living her life makes me the happiest person ever!

"Being a Swiftie in the United States is such fun! I love being able to talk to other Swifties on the Internet and then sometimes meet up with them at Taylor Swift events and concerts! We even video chat and have group chats sometimes. I just really love the things that Taylor can do and her power. Her fan base is unreal and so are the records she breaks! I will love Taylor forever and always."

Marley is twenty years old and from Piedmont, Alabama. Her favorite three songs are "All Too Well," "Tied Together With A Smile" and "Shake It Off." She says: "I love Taylor Swift for more reasons than I can even count. Her music saved my life from the very beginning. I started listening to her at fourteen years old, while learning how to drive for the first time, and I've loved her ever since. She is the most amazing role model and she has taught me so much about life and love. I never could repay her for all the things she has done for me, for all the ways she has helped me. That is why I'm such a loyal fan and that is why I will always have her back, because she's always had mine. She has been there for me when no one else has; she has been a huge constant in my life. It is amazing being a Swiftie in the US. I love interacting with all the other Swifties and going to concerts. I am actually friends with so many Swifties around the United States and around the world, thanks to social media. Taylor has brought us all together and I am so thankful for that."

Marley met Taylor on August 18, 2014 at her livestream in New York and then went back to her apartment for pizza! She had applied to attend the livestream, along with thousands of other Swifties, because it was an amazing opportunity. When she got the phone call from her management to say she had been chosen, she was blown away.

She explains: "After I hung up the phone, it all hit me in stages. First, was complete shock, I was at a loss for words. This was my dream and I could finally see that it was coming true: I was going to attend the livestream that I had thought about for weeks, the livestream that I was ecstatic about watching, let alone, attending. Second, was excitement—I was hugging my mother and thanking her for agreeing to make this once-in-a-lifetime trip with me. We both knew how much money it would cost, but my mom was willing to do it anyways. Everyone in my family knew my obsession with Taylor Swift, and they all promised me that they would do whatever it took for me to be able to meet her. As soon as I hung up the phone, I reminded my mom of when she said that, and then I said, 'You said *whatever*, right? Well, this is whatever.' "

Marley and her mom had to fly from Alabama to New York City at 6:00 a.m., but she was so excited, she wasn't sleepy. She was still really excited when she arrived at the hotel, and would have loved to chat to the other girls who were waiting in the lobby too but because they were all sworn to secrecy about the livestream no one dared say a word. Marley picks up her story: "None of us could mention the Taylor Swift livestream to anyone, so we all sat there until the two guys sitting at a table told us to form a line. I'm pretty sure we all knew who was a part of the eighty-nine, though. The girls and guys with the red Keds, dresses, red lipstick and cat shirts were definitely not at the hotel for a business meeting.

"We lined up, whispered 'Project Hummingbird' to the men at the tables and then we were escorted up an elevator to another floor. We had to hand over our belongings and a man with a metal detector scanned us up and down. Then we all piled into a room full of round tables and the chatting began. For a solid two hours, my table sat and talked about only Taylor Swift, it was like a Swiftie convention. Normal people would have been bored talking about a pop star for two hours solid, but not this fan base—we can talk about our queen for hours. The best part about being in this room full of strangers was that we all had one thing in common. Normally one thing wouldn't be a lot, but when that one thing is Taylor Swift, it is a big one thing.

"After a while, her management came in and told us it was time to walk over to the livestream, which would take place in the *Good Morning America* studios. Cool, huh? We all shuffled into the studio, grabbed the nearest couch, and watched the screen that counted down the minutes until we got to see Taylor. With sweaty palms and racing hearts, the clock finally hit one second. Suddenly a video of Taylor popped up on all the screens. A few seconds later, she entered the room, wearing a stunning white two-piece dress and red lipstick. All I remember is jumping up on the couch behind me and completely fangirling, which consisted of a few high-pitched shrieks and a bunch of *OMG*s.

"She sat up on the stage and released her album info, danced to her first single with us, and answered questions. She then had an interview with *Good Morning America* while we were all still in there. She referred to all eighty-nine of us as her 'biggest fans' and said we were her 'A Team.' That stuck, and so we all called ourselves 'Taylor's A Team' from then on. May I add, there were eighty-nine of us there and her album title is *1989* . . . She literally thinks of EVERYTHING. And we were informed later that she handpicked all of us and read every submission that we submitted. Only eighty-nine submissions were selected out of five thousand! It was definitely fate.

"Taylor also announced onstage that we were going to have a pizza party at a 'secure location.' I was sooooooo excited! When she'd finished, she came and took pictures with us in groups. Luckily, I was standing at the back of the group and that is exactly where she stood for the picture. So I scooted next to her as fast as I could and she put her arm around me to take the picture. I freaked . . . Like, seriously, I think my heart stopped for a good ten seconds while I smiled for the picture.

"After the picture she talked to us for a second. My brain was yelling, 'Say something, you dork!' but my mouth just wouldn't move. Luckily, I mustered up the courage to say, 'You are amazing, Taylor' as she walked by me. She seriously stopped in her tracks, turned around, made eye contact with me and said, 'Well, thank you.' Her smile was so big and so genuine. I mean, I was expecting just a simple thank you or sly smile, but she turned around and made complete eye contact with me. Oh, and just in case anyone is wondering, she is so flawless in person—there was not a blemish or bump on any part of her body. I mean, she looked just like a real-life Barbie doll, only more beautiful.

"She started to walk back up to the stage and I kind of reached out and touched her shoulder and said, 'Bye, Taylor.' She turned around and made eye contact again, and said, 'I'll see you again in, like, twenty-five minutes, at the party.' Our second conversation. I repeat, our second conversation. I just kept thinking to myself, *If these are the only two conversations I have with her today or ever, that will be okay because my dreams came true the minute she made eye contact with me*. That beautiful smile NEVER left her face the whole day. Kindness and grace just came so easily to her.

"After a while her management came and ushered us down to the charter buses to take us to the pizza party. We walked down about four flights of stairs. I'm not kidding you when I say that I fell down every single one of them. (Should've worn flats, but I had to be around Taylor's height!) We piled into charter buses to go to the 'unknown' location. We were all discussing the whole way there, 'like, what if the party is in her penthouse?' Then we decided not to get our hopes too high just in case it wasn't there.

"So we drove for about fifteen minutes and then turned on to Franklin Street in Tribeca and the bus shook. I mean, for a split second, there was an earthquake in New York City. I mean, all Swifties know that 155 Franklin Street is where Taylor lives, so as soon as we saw the sign, we knew. Part of me worried that the bus driver would just stop for a second and then drive on, but to my surprise he parked it on the curb right in front of her apartment.

"We were told to make a single file line by the stairs and that they would take us up in groups so we weren't all climbing the stairs at once. Finally, it was my turn to go up the treacherous, treacherous stairs in high heels. My calves were burning, but all I could think about was, *Taylor Swift is up there. I am about to walk into THE Taylor Swift penthouse!* I tripped a couple of times on my way up. Shocker! I finally made it up all the stairs in one piece and they told us to stand out in the hallway. I could hear her voice, but only barely, because the sound of my heartbeat was just so incredibly loud. Nervousness mixed with power walking up what felt like ten flights of stairs really does make your heart feel like it is beating out of your chest.

"The closer we got, her voice became more and more clear. Before I knew it, I was right outside her door. A girl right in front of me turned around and told me that Taylor was giving hugs to every single person. I knew right then and there that no day could top today.

"So I patiently waited for my time to get to meet her. I stepped inside her apartment, touched her door, of course (multiple times, no shame), and admired her decorations. The apartment was beautiful—it was like straight out of a catalog. When I walked in, I looked to the right and there was a big capital *T* with Christmas lights all over it and then there was a smaller *S* beside it. (Her initials, of course.) While I was admiring, Taylor kept saying, 'Come on in, you guys.' She said it so nonchalantly, like we were just her good friends coming over for a house party—it was the cutest thing ever. I could overhear her giving, like, legit life advice to every fan. It made my heart smile to know that she cared enough to hug each one of us and that she genuinely cared enough to listen to what we had to say and to give advice when we asked. I fell in love with her more when I saw how amazingly she treated us. She trusted us enough to let us in her house. There was maybe, like, one security guard, but no metal detectors. We could've taken anything, but Taylor trusted us, and it meant the world that she had willingly let us into her personal life.

"So back to the decorations . . . There was a bathroom and bedroom on the right, a black-and-white framed picture of Ed Sheeran giving the middle finger hanging on the wall, and two really cute velvet couches. On the left-hand side when you entered the door, there was a painting of Scott, her dad's, hand. So random, but I loved it because it was so something Taylor Swift would have in her NYC penthouse.

"So I finally get up to her. It was my chance to meet my idol. I had seen her in concert, on television, heard her on the radio, listened to her every day of my life on my iPod, and watched her cute video blogs on YouTube, but there she was, in the flesh. The girl that I have wanted to meet my entire life, the girl whose music saved my life, the girl whose words healed my heart and made me laugh and smile and cry: she was standing right in front of me. I had so many words that I wanted to say to her, but at that moment in time, nothing could come to mind.

"Me and two other girls stepped up and she hugged the two of them and then me. She pulled away and I blurted out, 'Thank you for spending your Monday night with us.' She didn't quite hear me (I probably stuttered), so she placed her hand on my arm and said, 'What?' And I repeated myself and she said, 'Oh, you're welcome! Thank *you.*' So I immediately told her about the song I wrote for her, just in case I forgot to mention it later on. I told her I wrote her a song called 'If You Don't Like Taylor Swift, You Should,' and she just smiled and said, 'Oh, yeah, thank you. I read all about it in your submission.' A smile so big crossed my face because I knew then that she really did read the submissions. There's no way she could've known I put it in there, if she didn't read ALL eighty-nine of the winning entries.

"Let me also add she was wearing a little black dress, she was barefoot, wore red lipstick, and had her hair fixed like it was for the livestream. Oh, and she was just casually drinking a Diet Coke while spitting out advice to us so good it could go in a book. So we stood there for another minute or two. I could tell she was a little overwhelmed because she had talked to and hugged, like, fifty people before me. She also looked at me and asked if I'd heard her song come on the radio a minute ago and we were all like, 'Yeah, we did!' She got all excited. I could just see her passion and love for her music in her eyes.

"She told one of the girls, 'I don't know what I'll be doing in four years' and I said, 'Well, you'll still be awesome, that's for sure.' And she looked at me and laughed. She asked me where I was from, probably because of the Southern accent, and then said something about how I came a long way. Then sadly the conversation had to come to an end and she said, 'Well, you guys go in the kitchen and have some pizza and drinks, I'll be in there in a minute.' Eating pizza and drinking Coke in T Swift's apartment, just a casual Monday night.

"So we walked into her living room and one of the girls called me over to look at Taylor's Grammy sitting on the table. I obviously touched it, and held it for a second. It seriously was SO much heavier than it looked. So then I made my way to the back of the living room to another room that looked somewhat like a sunroom. In it sat a beautiful piano. The first thing I wanted to do was play 'Love Story,' then 'All Too Well,' and then my Taylor Swift song, but unfortunately we weren't allowed to play it. So I just ran my fingers down the keys and sat on the bench. Just sitting in the exact spot she had sat many times before and playing a piano that she had written many hit songs on was a dream come true, especially for a pianist.

"Then I walked out and observed the sick pool table that was just casually chilling in her living room. I headed into the kitchen and decided to drink a Diet Coke for the very first time. It was only appropriate since she was, like, the face of Diet Coke, I was in her house, and she also was drinking one. Seriously, the best soda I ever had.

"About the time I picked up a drink, Taylor came in the kitchen and everyone piled in after her and crowded around her island in the middle of the kitchen. Well, I'm on the opposite side of her and little do I know sitting on the stool in front of me is Perez Hilton. I got up enough courage to tap him on the shoulder and tell him I watch his Instagram videos and that he has the cutest little boy ever. He smiled and thanked me.

"We were all kind of observing Taylor's every move while she picked up a piece of pizza. We just stood there in awe, like we had never seen someone eat a piece of pizza before. She was, like, 'I hate you all are having to watch me eat this piece of pizza so disgustingly.' (This is while she is trying to stop the cheese from falling off the pizza.) And we were all like, 'No, don't apologize, you are fine.' In all reality we were so enthused watching her eat the pizza. I mean, we had never seen Taylor Swift eat, let alone in her OWN apartment in NYC! So after she finished the pizza (she is a crust person, by the way—she ate the whole slice), she started talking to us again. We all chimed in with remarks and questions and as much as I wanted to bombard her with I love yous and questions, I didn't because I didn't want her to feel like she was at an interview. None of us really bombarded her. If anyone had walked in at that moment, they would have thought Taylor had thrown a pizza party for her closest friends.

"So someone brought up how skinny and good Tay looks, and I took my chance. I said, 'We now know how you keep your legs so toned. Walking up those stairs every day will do it, your secret is out!' Everyone in the room laughed and so did she. Then her song came on the radio. She froze for a second and then ran to turn it up and started freaking out and dancing to it. We all went crazy and so we had a dance party, in Taylor's kitchen, to her new single. Again, it was casual. When it was over she told us this was her first house party. I mean, what is life? I was at Taylor Swift's FIRST house party! A bunch of us got to talking and we were like, 'No one is ever going to believe us when we tell them this story.' Luckily, Taylor said, 'Where is my Polaroid?' She, like, made the camera sign with her hands and we all imitated because we REALLY wanted more pics with her, especially in her apartment. The lady was, like, 'Where is it?' And she was, like, 'in my room on my nightstand.'

"It was so great that the pictures were going to be made on a Polaroid, considering her album cover is a picture of her made on a Polaroid camera. No big deal! So Olivia Benson Swift wandered up and we all freak. Like that cat, number one, is SO cute and number two, kind of Twitter and Instagram famous. Meredith was kind of scared of us all, but Olivia let us pass her around. We also made Tay realize she released her single on 'Olivia Benson's birthday' and she was like, 'What? My cat?' And we were, like, 'No, the woman from *Law & Order SVU*' and she was, like, 'Oh, really? Well, I don't even have Olivia's papers so I wouldn't know. She was kind of handed to me.' The whole room burst out in laughter, of course.

"So here came Taylor into the living room with the Polaroid in hand. We all scooted closer to her and she was, like, telling us all to grab her Grammys off the tables and grab her VMA Award. We didn't hesitate. So we took pics with her, while we were holding her awards. I got a picture right beside her and I'm holding her Grammy and then in another pic I'm, like, two people away from her and I'm holding the VMA. She had a down moment, so I took another shot at saying something. I handed her the Grammy back and I said, 'This is heavy. It would hurt really bad if it fell on your toe.' She looked at it and then at me, and said, 'I think anything would hurt if you dropped it on your toe.' I had a conversation, with Taylor, about her Grammy. So cool!

"So unfortunately the time came for us to go and Taylor rushed to the door, where there was a ton of boxes. I rushed to the door behind her and I watched while she reached in the box and grabbed out a blue bag. She reached in it and started pulling out shirts. We all 'oohed' and 'ahed.' I remember saying, 'You shouldn't have, Taylor, this is enough, just being here.' And she kept digging and was like, 'It was nothing.' She was seriously so excited about the shirts, as were we, and her endless enthusiasm was just precious. There was a guy next to her handing out bags, so I kind of dodged him so she could hand me my gift bag and sure enough, she did. My final words were, 'It was so nice meeting you, Taylor, thank you so much.' Her response: 'Love you, babe.' Yep, my legs almost buckled and I had to steady myself down the flights of stairs because I knew if I got too excited, I would be going down them head first instead of feet first.

"8-18-14 was a DREAM COME TRUE for me. I was always terrified that I would never get to see Taylor, or hug her, or tell her thank you. I had prayed about meeting her every day of my life, and God made my dreams come true. I also have Taylor Nation to thank, and Taylor Swift for being such a kind-hearted person. She was everything I imagined she would be, and so much more. Meeting her was a day I will never forget, a day that I will tell my children about, my grandchildren about, and even random strangers who don't really care about. I'll never forget the feeling I felt that Monday. It was hands down THE best day of my life!

"People have asked me if I'm satisfied now that I have officially met my idol, checked out the number one thing on my bucket list, and fulfilled my dream, and of course my answer is YES! Because I am so very content with life right now. I have learned that dreams do come true, and if you want a dream bad enough and you fight hard enough for it, it can be yours.

"Will I be less obsessed with Taylor Swift because I met her? HECK NO! If anything, that Monday made me love her even more. How could you possibly stop obsessing over America's sweetheart? It's just not possible. I do have to make a new bucket list, though. Considering that 'Meet Taylor Swift' was all I had on it. Hmm . . . maybe I'll check off 'Meet Taylor Swift' and below it add 'Become Best Friends With Taylor Swift.'"

Marley has posted an incredible video on YouTube about her experience. Why not check it out by searching for "Marley Harper"?

New Yorkers Christina, who is twenty-one, and eighteen year-old Sanat are huge Taylor fans. They met on Taylor's online fan club, Taylor Connect, and instantly became friends in 2010. Finally, they met in person in 2012 and had a lot of fun during the *Red* release week. Christina's favorite three songs are "Style," "All Too Well" and "Our Song." Sanat's favorite songs are "This Love," "Ours" and "Holy Ground."

Christina explains how they came to meet Taylor: "When the Red Tour was announced, Sanat and I knew we wanted to go to a show together but because of conflicting schedules, we had to go to two separate shows. Later on, Taylor announced that she would be playing at the stadium near us, which was perfect! We decided that we were both going to go to that show together, but we waited to buy our tickets. About two weeks before the show, our local country radio station was giving out their last pair of tickets. I was out of the country on vacation so Sanat was the one calling in. Luckily, she was the right caller and we won the tickets! A few days later, they called Sanat back and told her they also wanted to give us meet-and-greet passes, which she kept a secret from me.

"The day of the show came and we got ready and headed to the venue early. Sanat had told me a fake story about how we had to pick something up at the box office. When we got there, she pulled out her camera and told me we were meeting Taylor. At that point I started hyperventilating and freaking out. After waiting in really long lines for ages, it was finally our turn to meet Taylor. As soon as she looked at me, she immediately opened her arms, welcoming me into a hug, and she did the same for Sanat, who was behind me. She was quick to compliment us on our homemade costumes and she was so easy to talk to. We got so wrapped up in talking to her that we had to be reminded to take a picture. We were even rushed out of there because we were taking too long. As soon as I walked out, I was in awe of the entire experience. I can't thank Sanat enough for what she did for me and we are both grateful we got to experience it together.

"There are many things we love about Taylor, but we think the one thing about her that stands out for us is how she treats us. We love how she treats us more like friends than fans. When we were talking to her, she made us feel so comfortable and like we'd known her for years. You don't get that feeling with many celebrities."

Jessica is fifteen and from Valliant, Oklahoma. Her three favorite songs are "Enchanted," "Dear John" and "Bad Blood." Her favorite videos are *Tim McGraw* and *Fifteen* because they are so deep and meaningful. She says: "I love being a fan in [the US] because there are so many fangirls everywhere that my love for Taylor Swift doesn't seem that crazy.

"I was fortunate enough to meet Taylor in Loft 89 with my sister and I've posted a video on my YouTube channel [Jessica Stuart] to describe what happened and offer advice to other Swifties who dream about meeting Taylor one day. Why don't you check it out?

"I never expected to be chosen for Loft 89 because we had horrible seats, at the top, at the very back . . . but we were. During the seventh song, 'I Know Places,' we were singing and dancing when Andrea [Taylor's mom] approached us and invited us to go to Loft 89. We couldn't believe it because normally she picks people during the last song. The rest of the concert was a blur, we were so excited.

"When we went to Loft 89, a lady explained that we could take as many photos as we liked, but we couldn't take any videos. A few people tried to sneak in without orange wristbands, but security was tight, so they were turned away.

"It looked amazing inside, like a New York apartment. Taylor was so lovely. We chatted, posed for a photo and she signed my ticket for me. She wrote 'I heart Jessica' on it and I know I'll keep it forever.

"If I was to give anyone any advice on how to get into Loft 89, I would say, try to stand out. We had signs with lights on them; my sister's poster broke so she wrapped the lights around her body. We didn't know, but you could see her from right at the bottom. At the end of the day, if you want to be noticed you've got to dance, sing and have fun. Don't sit down, dance like crazy, put effort into your posters! I will never forget the emotions I felt that night, it was the best night of my life."

Gianna is fifteen and from Paramus, New Jersey. Her favorite three songs are "Tim McGraw," "Fearless" and "Wish You Would." She says: "What I love most about Taylor is how inspirational she is, she is an amazing role model for so many people. She is also so relatable and understanding to so many different people. There is always a song for whatever I'm going through that helps me and I know that many other people feel this way.

"To be a fan in America is amazing, but it's also very difficult because she does get a lot of hate and that is hard to hear at times. It's great to spend time with other Swifties and go to concerts because when you're with Swifties you can just feel the love and support for her.

"I have been a Taylor Swift fan for as long as I can remember, and I have been to every single tour—Fearless, Speak Now, Red and now 1989. Throughout the tours I have been seated in all different places, but for the 1989 Tour we were the furthest we have ever been: we were in the very last section they sold tickets for! Although I wasn't thrilled about our seats, my two friends, my sister and I still got completely dressed up for Taylor. We were in tutus and glowsticks and made huge posters, we were so excited. Taylor finally opened after we got there early and waited for her for three hours and it was . . . FLAWLESS! 'Welcome to New York' was fantastic, especially with the glowing bracelets that magically turned on when she came out. My friends and I were going crazy, dancing and singing as loud as we could, even though everyone else in our section was sitting.

"During the second song, a lady with just a badge and a concert shirt came up to me and asked, 'Would you like to sit closer to Taylor?' and my immediate answer was 'YES!' and she then told us we had front-row tickets, then I looked down and we were seated on the floor, in the FIRST row! I grabbed my friends and started running frantically down three flights of stairs until we got to the floor. And the guards just kept telling us keep going, keep going, keep going! I had tears in my eyes—it was so incredible, especially because I had never been on the floor before. Finally, there were no more chairs . . . we were literally the front row! In the seat next to us was a nice woman and her cousin, and we danced and sang with them throughout the whole concert (which still leaves me speechless!) and she told us that this was the friends and family section. And we came to realize at the end of the night that she was *The Bachelorette*, Andi Dorfman, from Season 13. And we had no idea it was her the whole night! It was the most surreal thing that had ever happened, it was something out of a movie, and we are so grateful that happened to us and this is why we love Taylor as much as we do . . . she truly makes dreams come true."

Kristen is nineteen and from Bloomfield, New Jersey. Her favorite three songs are "Ours," "Change" and "Clean." She loves Taylor "because she is real, and stands true to who she is and what she stands for, and that makes her a true role model. Plus, she speaks on behalf of girls all over the world, and personally connects to each and every fan. Her love for us is what makes us support her and love her even more. Finally, being a Swiftie in the US means I'm very lucky. There are so many opportunities to try to see Taylor, and the Swiftie fan base is very strong and supportive as well."

Here, she shares her story: "On October 3, 2014, I was fortunate to be picked to attend the 1989 Secret Session in Taylor's apartment in Soho! Before I explain that day, it is important I say WHY I was picked. Now, the majority of the fans who were chosen were chosen because they have very large fan-based sites or social media accounts and showed daily how dedicated to Taylor they were. Now, though I am as big a fan as them, I was picked because of a picture. My best friend Sam won pit seats for the Red Tour for the Prudential Center, and took me. When the day came, I was a mess and full of energy and shaking from excitement, knowing how close I would be to my idol. After waiting in line for five hours, we were lucky enough to secure a spot right along the catwalk and my nerves kicked in even more. I cannot explain why, but when I get starstruck or really happy, or excited, I begin to shake. Once the concert began and the big RED letters went up and Taylor's silhouette appeared, I started freaking out! Second song in, during 'Holy Ground,' Taylor reached down and touched my hand, looking me in the eyes and I LOST it. For the rest of the concert I started screaming, crying and shaking uncontrollably—I actually looked like a crazy person.

"Six months after the concert, I got a tweet asking if this extremely unattractive girl freaking out at a Taylor Swift concert was me, and it was. It turns out NJ.com posted an article about the tour and pictures of me were all over it. Someone made a meme and it went VIRAL in the Swiftie community on Tumblr, Twitter and Instagram. I was so embarrassed at first as more and more people found out it was me, but time went on and I learned to embrace this picture.

"Fast forward two years, and October 1, 2014, I received a phone call from TaylorSwift.com. I was in complete shock and started crying, again, on the phone with them. They ended up telling me I was invited to this top-secret event. I could tell no one but one emergency contact, and I only knew the meeting place. When I got off the phone, I was in such shock; I called my mom, who would be my emergency contact. I was crying so much that she was scared at first. When I told her about what was happening, she started to cry too, knowing it was my dream to meet the person I have looked up to for almost ten years! During the phone call I asked if my best friend Sam could go, because our friendship started from Taylor and she took me to all Taylor's concerts. They unfortunately told me no. However, the next day, Sam got a phone call inviting her to go and it made the day even more special.

"On the Friday I was meeting Taylor, I had to leave college early but couldn't tell anyone where I was going. All my friends were confused about why I skipped class and just left. (They would soon find out when they went on social media that night and saw Polaroids of me and Taylor!)

"I went to the mall to buy an outfit that would go with my Red Taylor Swift Keds, curled my hair and went to the city with my mom and Sam. We ending up arriving at our meeting spot two hours early and that was the longest two hours of my life! We aimlessly roamed until 3:00 p.m. came and we went inside to find fans; you could tell we were Swifties (we all have a certain style and vibe to us that make us the best and most supportive fan group). Once inside, we had to wait for a little bit then went into this room, where we signed two contracts, were checked by security and had to put our valuables away. Sam and I were in Group 2, and I remember sitting in this room full of excited fans, unsure of the day's events, and thinking, *Why am I so calm? I hope I appreciate the moment and don't let it pass.*

"Sam just laughed at me, knowing I wouldn't be calm for long, and she was right because once Groups 1–5 were called onto the bus, I started shaking and crying AGAIN. We arrived at her apartment and when we first entered, everyone got so excited and we were all squealing. Little did we know that was her security guard's apartment. We walked into Taylor's hallway and it was lined with pictures, and once we entered her living room, everyone's jaws dropped. It was PERFECTION, and something that looked like it came straight from [the store] Anthropologie. There was a table of food with sushi, chicken, pizza, and so much more. We were allowed to walk around the first floor and see her Grammys and VMAs and her piano. It was so much to take in; everyone was almost silent from awe. It is a funny sight to see Swifties in Taylor's bathroom, making mental notes of what soap and shampoo she uses. There were giant throw pillows on the floor and a big chair with speakers that we assumed Taylor would be sitting in, so Sam and I took the first pillow and ending up being inches from Taylor all night!

"The rest of the groups came in and once everyone got settled, all of a sudden we heard 'Hey, guys!' and, looking like an angel, she floated into the room and everyone started crying. I remember tissues being thrown all over and everyone holding each other and it was the definition of a Kodak moment. Taylor sat down and after talking to us for a little she explained every song and I swore I was in a dream. For a moment it seemed like everything paused in my head and I remember thinking to take all of this in because it is truly once in a lifetime!

"When Taylor explained every song, she would do it with such passion and enthusiasm, and while the songs were playing she would do, like, a little dance in her chair and mouth all the words. During all the songs Taylor consistently made eye contact with us and would have a moment with everyone there. It was magical! Around the fourth song, I hadn't stopped crying at that point. I felt a sob slip out as my shaking continued and Taylor stopped mid-conversation and looked at me. She asked if I was okay and said she was concerned about my shaking, but after being assured that I was just REALLY excited, she gave me a high-five, which made me cry more. We got halfway through the album and Taylor said it's time for a break. She took off her five-inch Louis Vuitton heels, hopped on her chair and blasted 'Shake It Off,' starting a dance party! (Yes, I shook it off to 'Shake It Off' with Taylor Swift!) Taylor went through the room, dancing with everyone.

"We got to stroke her cat Olivia, and Taylor brought out DELICIOUS chocolate-chip cookies and heart-shaped Rice Krispies dipped in chocolate. The thing that was amazing was no one crowded Taylor—they let her roam as she wished and never got jealous if she was with someone else. During this mini-intermission a mom who was there came up to me and said, 'I was talking to Taylor's guard and he said that he has been with Taylor for a long time, but out of everyone, YOU take the cake!' My heart melted a little inside from excitement.

We went through the second half of the CD and then it was one-on-one time.

"As we waited for our turn her mom walked around, talking to everyone, and she is sooooo sweet! Fast forward a little, Sam talked to Taylor first and they took a cute pose on the steps, holding Grammys, and then the three of us got to take a 'best friends' picture together! Then it was my turn and I wasn't sure if I would hold it together or not. I gave her a hug and thanked her a million times, asked for some advice, and she told me that one of the first things she thought when she saw me was that I was beautiful. No matter how hard I tried, this made me cry. It was amazing to know that she would take as long as I wanted and it felt in no way rushed. I told her about this pose I wanted to do for our picture where we held hands, lifted one leg up and went on our other tippy toe. She said she loved it! Finally, I asked if I was picked because of the picture and she said, 'Yeah, I'm a sucker for that stuff!'

"I left Taylor's apartment and met everyone in the security guard's living room again. Once I entered, everyone cheered because somehow I made it through the night without passing out. We were given a gorgeous canvas tote with about $250 worth of stuff inside. When we went back on the bus and arrived at the meeting place again my mom was waiting there, smiling from ear to ear in excitement for us. That night, my social media sites were flooded with comments and likes about the night and when I went back to college, everyone wanted to know what happened!

"If there is one thing I could wish for, it would be to PROPERLY thank Taylor, for not only what she has done for me personally but for Swifties all over the world. October 3, 2014 will forever be the best day in my life and I vow to forever be a Swiftie!"

Rachel is nineteen and from Goffstown, New Hampshire. Her favorite three songs are "Red," "Our Song" and "Shake It Off." She says: "I love 'Red' because it tells a beautiful story, 'Our Song' because it was the first Taylor track I had ever heard (and eventually became obsessed with), and 'Shake It Off' is something fresh and new, explaining how you just have to stay true to yourself. All of her music is A plus, but these three, in my opinion, cover a lot of T Swizzle ground.

"The thing I love about Taylor the most is that she is such a genuine person. Tay genuinely cares about her friends, family, her fans, writing and producing her own music, and putting on an incredible show throughout her tours. When she looks out into the crowd and smiles, you know it is one hundred percent pure happiness and gratitude to be doing what she loves.

"It's very cool to be a Swiftie in the US, because many of my friends, family, and coworkers love her, too. She is obviously very well known, and it's amazing that I've been lucky enough to see her in concert two times at Gillette Stadium (once at the Red Tour, once for the 1989 World Tour). Being a Swiftie in 2015 also means you can easily connect to other fans around the country, and even across the world, who are just as obsessed as you are.

"I first became a fan of T Swizz around 2009 when Taylor's 'Love Story' became super popular. That's when I started to listen to her music more, and purchased her album *Fearless* on iTunes.

"My favorite music video is *Red*. Although it's not your 'typical' music video, I love the montages of different parts of the Red Tour. It gives me chills every single time I watch it. What a masterpiece!

"Attending the 1989 World Tour was the most amazing experience of my life. It was without a doubt the best concert I've ever been to. Taylor puts on an amazing show, and the wristbands that light up to every song were a really nice touch. Taylor definitely knows how to enhance the whole concert experience for everyone. Of course there were lots of lights, special effects, fireworks, and plenty of singing and dancing. One of my favorite performances was the rock version of 'We Are Never Ever Getting Back Together.' I absolutely love that song, and the rock spin on it was incredible!

"Taylor's outfits were stunning (as always). From sparkly pink skirts that light up, to rocking jet-black pieces, Tay has worn it all. One of my favorite outfits was the one she wore during 'Shake It Off,' which was a deep blue sparkly top and matching skirt. It was so cute and it fit her personality so well. And obviously, it looked cool when she 'shook off' all her troubles and danced around the stage! Taylor, her crew, and the entire stadium got to dance the night away together in screaming color. Another INSANE aspect of the finale during 'Shake It Off' was the fact that the catwalk lifted up and spun around! So cool!

"In addition to this craziness, the night I attended the tour, Taylor brought out a special guest, Walk the Moon, to sing 'Shut Up And Dance'! It was tons of fun singing along and dancing to the track. It's a night I will remember forever because the concert was everything my 'wildest dreams' are made of.

"I could go on and on about Taylor, but the bottom line is that I will always love her music. It's so moving, relatable and fun, and I'm pretty sure I will continue to love every beautiful song she writes. I really hope I get to meet her one day."

Breanna is seventeen and from Dracut, Massachusetts. Her favorite three songs are "Long Live," "All Too Well" and "You're In Love." She says: "I love how much I can relate to Taylor's songs, how much emotion she puts into every song. Since becoming a fan I've wanted to be like her—she doesn't care what anyone thinks of her, she does what she pleases. I just want to be as genuinely happy as she is. She really is inspiration. For me, the best part of being a fan is when she's onstage and talking to the crowd you can tell how much she loves what she does by the HUGE smile on her face.

"Being a fan in the USA is memorable because she started her career here, so there's a lot of places that mean a lot to her—for example, when I see her in concert, it's at Gillette Stadium, and that was the first stadium she sold out—and every time I've been there it always rains and we all dance in the rain together, singing at the top of our lungs.

"I've never met Taylor herself, but at the Red Tour, I met Andrea Swift (Momma Swift) and at the 1989 Tour, I met Taylor's guitarist, Paul Sidoti. I think when you go to a concert, you should always keep your eyes peeled. I spotted Andrea when Taylor was performing 'Love Story'—I was just singin g and dancing along with my friend when I saw her. We went over to introduce ourselves and gave her a hug; it was really nice. We spotted Paul when he was taking two girls to their seats in the pit at the 1989 show, so we went over to say hello.

I'm so glad we did because he was lovely and he happily posed for a picture with us. All of Tay's family, friends and band members are super friendly, so you should never be afraid to say a quick hello. They really appreciate all our support."

Regina is twenty and from Connecticut. Her favorite songs are "Last Kiss," "Fearless" and "Clean." She explains: " 'Last Kiss' is beautifully written and musically satisfying. When I first listened to her *Speak Now* album, 'Last Kiss' is one of the songs I played over and over. I was used to Taylor's upbeat songs and this, being over six minutes long, was anything but upbeat. 'Last Kiss' is raw emotion, and I'm thankful Taylor shared it with the world.

"Another favorite of mine is 'Fearless' because of its fun and innocent lyrics. It is a good song to listen to while you are enjoying the moment you're in, and, for once, not worrying about tomorrow. 'Clean' has to be my favorite song from the *1989* album. It applies to the situations where you need that extra push to help you get over something that's been nagging or keeping happiness from your life. Listen to this song and release what's been weighing you down!

"My favorite music video to date is *The Best Day* because it shows home videos of Taylor growing up. The song is about growing up with someone (in Taylor's case, it was her mom), who's always been there for you. I love this music video because it shows Taylor as a baby, a toddler, and eventually as a teenager playing her guitar in her living room. The video is very different from her other videos. It's a light-hearted video that many people can relate to, if they are lucky enough to have someone by their side.

"One of the many things I love most about Taylor is her style. She somehow has a certain way about her with every album she releases. Her hair, clothes, and overall 'look' almost match the emotions in her albums. I think this is a positive quality in her. She keeps us interested in what she's going to wear next. Will it be curly hair, a cute sundress and a floral headband? Or straight hair, a pair of shorts and a crop top? Throughout these style changes, she has never changed her quirky and gracious personality (another thing I love about her).

"Being a Taylor Swift fan in the United States of America is extra special because Taylor lives here! I am honestly very lucky to be in the country where Taylor spends a lot of her time, writes many of her songs, and meets her fans along the way.

"I am also lucky because I was given the opportunity to attend one of the 1989 Secret Sessions at Tay's home in Rhode Island. To listen to the album a month before its release was incredible. Taylor talked, laughed and danced with us. She even passed around homemade cookies and Rice Krispies Treats. I met Taylor's mother, Andrea, and her father, Scott. Scott gave me two guitar picks! I walked up to Andrea, where a few other people were standing. Andrea asked each of us of our names, hugged us, and said Taylor was so excited about these 'secret sessions.'

"When I met Taylor she smiled widely and said, 'Hi! Glad you could be here!' Imagine, Taylor Swift being glad I could make it to her house! A lot of what we talked about is a blur to me—I was so starstruck! I do remember her thanking me, and I thanking her. She said, 'Well, I'll see you at a show or something?' I replied, 'Yes!' This has since come true. In July of 2015, I was able to see her perform during her 1989 Tour at Gillette Stadium in Massachusetts.

"Taylor met every single fan that was at her house that night. She took her time with each of us, and we were able to have a Polaroid picture taken with her! In my Polaroid, Taylor is hugging me and I'm holding one of her (several) Grammy Awards! I will forever remember that night, a complete surprise, when Taylor Swift opened her home to me, shared her music and her kind hospitality."

Caroline is seventeen and from Portland, Maine. She says: "My favorite songs are 'Never Grow Up,' because I have such a personal connection to the song and it makes me think about my childhood, 'I Wish You Would' and 'Superstar.' I first latched onto 'I Wish You Would' when Taylor used my pictures on Twitter during release week with the caption 'I'll never forget you as long as I live,' and ever since I've seen it on tour, my love has grown because it's a really fun song to experience live. I know that 'Superstar' may not be a popular answer but I think any fan of any artist can connect to it. Whenever I hear 'Superstar,' it just takes me back to 'Fearless' days when I first started loving Taylor and I think about how I used to dream about meeting her or even seeing her live. Now thinking about how far I have come in the realm of things (meeting her twice, being followed, reblogged, *taylurked*, etc.), I look back at the twelve-year-old who had her walls covered top to bottom with Taylor posters and I get really happy.

"My favorite music video has to be *Mine*. Being from Maine, I can answer this question without thinking twice.

Mine was filmed about twenty minutes south of my city, so I visit that town a lot. I've been to just about every spot in the music video, so it's really cool to watch it and know the stories behind every shot.

"I think the thing I love about Taylor the most is her care and dedication for her fans. Not many artists spend their free time online learning as much as possible about their fans' lives. She really wants to get to know her fans on a different level, and that's an amazing thing for her to do, especially at her level of fame and success. I consider myself very lucky to be a Swiftie living in the US. Taylor does the most shows here, lives here, and is in the same time zone (which is very helpful for Tumblr).

"In October 2014, I was fortunate enough to go to NYC for the weekend of *1989*'s release. On October 26, the day before *1989* came out, about fifty Swifties from Twitter and Tumblr met up in Central Park to film a music video to 'Welcome to New York.' It was the best part of my trip because I got to meet so many people that I've become close friends with online. It was like we were in our own little world—just us, Central Park, and 'W2NY' on repeat for two hours. It was an experience unlike anything I've ever done, and I'm so glad I was a part of it.

"The next day, at 3:30 a.m., I woke up and took the subway to Times Square to go to *Good Morning America*. Taylor was there to promote *1989*, so my friend and I went and waited outside against the barricade. We were right at the front, so when Taylor came out to see fans . . . WE MET HER! It was fifteen seconds of pure joy and happiness. I got a selfie and she signed the poster I made, and somehow in a twist of fate, *Good*

Morning America took a video and an HQ candid shot of me meeting her. I still can't believe how lucky I am. The next day, when I went home and went to school, everyone was talking to me about it— even my teachers and coaches—and it just felt truly amazing.

"In June 2015, I was fortunate enough to take a trip down to Philadelphia to stay with some of my best friends and go to Tay's concert with them. It was, hands down, the greatest night of my life because I finally got to meet people who have been a part of my life for years now. There were SO many Twitter friends at the Taylor Nation booth, we flooded it with sing-alongs and photo shoots. Oh yeah, and the girls I went with? We also got Loft 89 together. In a crazy twist of fate our group of four went to Loft 89, where we got to talk with the one and only Taylor Swift.

"I couldn't believe it was actually happening, and I still can't believe it happened. We had so much fun talking to Taylor. She is as nice, funny, and caring as everyone says she is. We all took our pictures with her, and mine was a pose based on our undeniable height difference. I go up to her and say, 'My Twitter name is CantReachCarol, so could we do a pose where I can't reach you?' and she happily agreed. We were struggling at first, but we finally figured it out. It was so fun to live through that with her by my side, and now whenever I meet other Swifties we do that pose together. That night, I also got to meet Andrea and her special guest singer, Rachel Platten. It was a night I'll never forget and I can't thank Taylor enough."

Julia is fifteen and from Allentown, Pennsylvania. Her favorite songs are "Enchanted," "All Too Well," "Teardrops On

My Guitar" and "Wildest Dreams." She says: "In the USA, we are all positively mad for Taylor, especially living in her home state. I've seen her six times in concert and she is astonishing every single time. We love her so, so much!

"I first fell in love with Taylor when I was about seven years old and I first heard 'Tim McGraw' and 'Teardrops On My Guitar,' and from there, I totally lost it for her. She blew me away, even at that age, with her way of telling a story and putting such honest thought into her lyrics. Since then I've plastered her face on my walls, bought every song and listened to every interview. I even learned how to play guitar and now I write songs as well to cope with everyday, or not-so-everyday, events in my life.

"She's influenced me so much and I will always treasure that. I love Taylor's ability to captivate people, and to really make them feel a connection to her. I truly feel that for the longest time Taylor has been my best friend and she will always be, and for that I owe her the world.

"My favorite music video Taylor has ever put out would have to be the one for *I Knew You Were Trouble*. It's an excellent song and the video is so real and honest. It has a beautiful intro, explaining what she went through, that sets the mood just perfectly, and then she takes you through the toxic relationship and it's heart wrenching. It's such a moving and intricate masterpiece put into just a couple minutes. I like most of her videos but this one has always stuck with me.

"I love seeing Tay perform live. All of her performances are amazing; it's almost theatrical. My favorite tour would have to be the Speak Now World Tour. The whole feeling of the show was so romantic and dreamy. She made sure to pay attention to the full audience by having her small stage in the back and there, she sang some old songs, new ones and covers. It feels like she's just sitting there and singing to you—not putting on an act or anything, just being her own amazing self, feeling the music. I truly believe no matter what boys come and go in her life, music will always be the love of her life. It's just beautiful to hear her do what she loves. She's astonishing."

CHAPTER 4

AUSTRALIA

The first time Taylor toured Australia was in March 2009. Back then, she wasn't very well known and her performance at the Tivoli Theater in Brisbane only drew a crowd of fifty to a hundred people. She sang "You Belong With Me," "Our Song," "Tell Me Why," "Teardrops On My Guitar," "Forever And Always," "Hey Stephen," "White Horse," "Leavin'," "Should've Said No," "Fearless," "Tim McGraw," "Love Story," "Change" and "Picture To Burn."

Since then, Taylor has gained thousands of fans in Australia, and in February 2010 she performed her Fearless show in Brisbane, Sydney, Newcastle, Melbourne and Adelaide. She was back in Australia in March 2012 with her Speak Now World Tour and again in December 2013 with Red. Taylor has always appreciated the support that Australian Swifties give her and was so excited for them to see her 1989 show in November and December 2015. She actually finished the tour at the AAMI Park in Melbourne.

When she came to Australia in March 2012, she enjoyed spending quality time with her family. She went to the beach with her brother Austin, walked along the sands and enjoyed a cooked breakfast at Bill's Cafe in Surry Hills. She also went on a yacht ride to see the Sydney Opera House and Sydney Harbour Bridge up close and took her dad out for dinner on his sixtieth birthday.

On March 7, she tweeted: "Both shows in Brisbane were magical and wildly dancy. And so completely worth the trip."

Taylor always has an intense schedule, so she has to take advantage of any days off. She told *Glamour* magazine back in 2009: "On any given day I do five or six different interviews. If we are somewhere really pretty, I'll try to experience the place I'm in. Today, I'm going to head to the beach. My meet-and-greet schedule starts at 5:00 p.m. The show starts at 8:00 p.m. Then, I'll do a mass meet and greet with people who won a radio contest, or who we found in the nosebleed section.

"I am a workaholic. I get really restless when I haven't worked for a day and a half. I have a recurring dream that people are lined up next to my bed, waiting for autographs and taking pictures of me!"

She has also admitted in the past that music is her boyfriend: "I don't date a lot. The other day I was in my dressing room with one of my closest friends, Kellie Pickler, who is also my opening act, and she said something really interesting to me: 'We can only give someone what's left over.' She does the same thing I do, so she knows what it's like to do interviews all day and give your heart and soul onstage every night. After all of that is taken, we can only give someone what's left. So it's hard."

At her Brisbane Red show on December 7, 2013, there was a minor staging collapse but Taylor took it in her stride, chatting to her audience in darkness until the problem was fixed. Some fans were disappointed, as they had to move seats so missed some of the show, but they were offered a refund later.

In an interview with Australian radio show, *Jules, Merrick & Sophie*, Taylor revealed: "The most important thing for me is maintaining artistic integrity, which means as a songwriter I still continue to write about my life."

When asked to talk about the critics who say she only writes about her past relationships, she replied: "Frankly, I think that's a very sexist angle to take. No one says that about Ed Sheeran. No one says that about Bruno Mars. They're all writing songs about their exes, their current girlfriends, their love life, and no one raises a red flag there."

Taylor couldn't wait to visit Australia for her 1989 Tour. She told ARIA Charts that aside from entertaining her fans she was planning on: "Beach. Shopping. Restaurants. You guys have amazing food. Kangaroos. I love kangaroos."

They asked her the best way she's celebrated a chart success and she replied: "Honestly I just like to get my friends together and either have dinner or have a dance party. I think that, for me, last night was the perfect example because at the Billboard Awards we all had such an amazing time. The performance was something we were really proud of and a lot of my friends were there. We all went out for dinner afterward—it was me and Selena and Ed and a bunch of people we tour with and dancers. It ended up being a great thing, people would text and come out and hang out with us, and I love it when you have a bunch of people in one place and everybody just ends up converging."

In January 2015, Taylor's fans campaigned to get her in radio station Triple J's Hottest 100 chart as they were annoyed that "Shake It Off" didn't receive a single play on Triple J in 2014 and so wasn't included in their list of aired songs for Hottest 100 voting. The station did allow listeners to nominate any song they liked, so Swifties campaigned hard to try to get "Shake It Off" to the top of the list. Triple J is an indie radio station, so some of its fans did respond negatively to the campaign, but Australian Swifties just shook it off. The #Tay4Hottest100 campaign went viral on social media, but sadly, Triple J made the decision to disqualify "Shake It Off" from the competition, which was a big blow to Swifties.

Louisa is eighteen and from Sydney. Her favorite three songs are "All Too Well," "Mean" and "Shake It Off." She says: "To be a Swiftie in Australia is amazing because Australia loves Taylor Swift. It's so cool to meet up with other Swifties and she tours here, which is great. I have friends from other countries too, thanks to Taylor. I'm really close to a fan from Scotland called Danielle.

"When she performed her Red Tour in Brisbane I went with my sisters, Ruby, Tab, Kayla and Steph, and Max, my brother—we all love her so it was nice that we could experience the show together. My favorite bits of the concert were when Taylor talked to us in between songs. When she speaks, it's like she's talking to you personally and everything she says is so relatable and inspirational, just like her lyrics. They're perfection.

"During the concert some of the lights onstage broke and for about ten minutes she was just talking to us like we had all been friends for a long time. She talks to us as friends, not as fans. She could have left the stage and had a break while they fixed the problem but she didn't, she just wanted us to have the best experience and so just chatted to us.

"Every song she sang that night was done perfectly. The performances were amazing. It was the best night of my life. I loved it when Taylor did the Aussie chant 'Aussie, Aussie, Aussie!'—and then she held the microphone out to us as we said, 'Oi, Oi, Oi!' The crowd went wild."

Doug is from Wodonga, Victoria. He is forty-seven and his favorite songs are "Long Live," "State Of Grace" and "New Romantics." He says: "I become a fan after listening to 'Long Live' on the radio in the car. I asked my kids who it was singing and they said Taylor. This was about the time she had released *Red* or around the start of the *Red* era. I bought that album and that was it. I have been a Swiftie ever since.

"The *1989* era is just awesome . . . my favorite video has to be *Bad Blood*. I like it because it celebrates being broken but that sticking together with our friends, we can become a force to be reckoned with. We can overcome anything.

"I might be older than a typical Swiftie (and male) but Taylor's music is so incredible that it appeals to people of all ages. I think it's great that she's such an awesome role model for young girls and she is so generous to her fans. She isn't a diva and appreciates every single fan who supports her.

"She has a great fan base in Australia and we support her in everything she does. It is a bit harder being a guy Swiftie because there aren't many of us around. I know that I'll probably never get the opportunity to meet Taylor in person because she doesn't visit Australia very often, but I'm okay with that."

CHAPTER 5

BELGIUM

Taylor loved visiting Belgium in March 2011 and told her Twitter followers: "Belgium is cool!" Belgium Swiftie Célestine replied: "Yes, it is!! So come back? Please!! Can't wait to see you, Tay!"

She didn't bring her Fearless Tour to Belgium but Taylor did bring her Speak Now World Tour to the Forest National in Brussels on March 6. Her supporting act was Flemish singer Tom Dice. Over 4,500 fans got to see Taylor perform that night but sadly she didn't return with her Red or 1989 shows. Taylor would love to visit Belgium again but because she is so popular around the world, she finds it hard to visit every country.

She is so grateful that some of her biggest Belgium Swifties make the trip to other countries to see her perform and likes hearing from them how things are going in Belgium. And she is always thankful to the fans who buy her music, because they help make her dreams come true.

DID YOU KNOW?

"Picture To Burn" from Taylor's first album, *Taylor Swift*, was about a guy who made her angry because he didn't like her back. She still doesn't think the guy she wrote about realizes that the song is about him. Another song from the album about unrequited love is "Teardrops On My Guitar," which was written about Tay's friend Drew Chadwick. She mentions him by name so there was no confusion about whom she was singing once the album was released.

Aurélie is twenty and from Brussels. She was watching a music video channel called MCM when she saw Taylor's music video for "Love Story" for the first time. Aurélie can remember it clearly; it was a Saturday morning in 2008 and she's been a Swiftie ever since.

She says: "I love all her songs because they are so unique and beautiful. Obviously, 'Love Story' has a special place in my heart but I also love 'Tim McGraw' and 'The Best Day.'

"I love *The Best Day* video. I think it's really adorable that Taylor has shared special moments from her life with us. I think the video for '22' is so much fun, it's so colorful and lets us see what it'd be like to be Tay's friend in real life.

"Nothing compares to seeing Tay perform live. I've seen her perform her Speak Now World Tour in my home country and I've been to see her 1989 World Tour in Amsterdam and Dublin. She's an incredible performer.

"I'd like her to perform more shows in Belgium, but even if she doesn't, I'll travel thousands of miles to see her again. I'll be a Swiftie forever."

Febe is fifteen and from Brussels. She says: "I love all of Tay's songs and my favorites change every month. At the minute, I'd say my favorite three were 'Love Story,' 'Haunted' and 'I Know Places.' I fell in love with Taylor, listening to 'Love Story' so it's always been special to me. I think 'Haunted' is a great song and not many people have listened to it. It's from Taylor's third album, *Speak Now*, which was released in 2010. If you haven't listened to it, you should—it deserves to be loved. 'I Know Places' is a cool song and it makes me happy, so it's in my top three.

"My favorite video has to be *The Best Day* because it's made from lots of her home videos. I love seeing Taylor when she was little and seeing Andrea and Scott enjoying watching their lovely girl play. I find it really tugs on my heartstrings because you know it's not acting—it's her real life.

"I love being a Swiftie, but it isn't easy being a fan here in Belgium. The Swifties I know live far away, so we have to communicate online rather than face to face. I wish it was easy to buy Taylor merchandise here, but it's not—the only stuff available tends to be from the Speak Now Tour because this was the last time she visited Belgium. I really hope she comes back one day. I'd love to meet her and thank her for being my inspiration."

CHAPTER 6

BRAZIL

Taylor didn't bring her Fearless, Speak Now, Red or 1989 Tours to Brazil, but she did a micro tour of Brazil in 2012, which included an exclusive performance in Rio de Janeiro. During her show at the Citibank Hall, she brought South American country star Paula Fernandes on to the stage to sing "Long Live" with her.

DID YOU KNOW?

Paula Fernandes had recorded a Portuguese version of the song a few months earlier, but this was the first time they'd ever sung together. It was a beautiful performance, with Paula singing the verses in Portuguese and Taylor singing the chorus in English.

While in Brazil, Taylor attended a press conference at the Sofitel Hotel in Rio de Janeiro.

She was presented with a Gold Record Award and afterwards signed autographs and posed for photographs with the fans waiting outside. Afterwards she tweeted, "I love Brazil," and it was retweeted over 46,000 times.

Many Swifties communicate online via social media, and Brazilian Swifties are no exception. Taylor loves using social media herself but always wants her fans to be careful when they're making friends online. In 2007 she joined a campaign to raise awareness of online predators and reminded fans at a special event that: "when you meet somebody online, you can never really know them. If there are two or three of you here that maybe would get lonely after school, and somebody random [instant messages] you and says that they're a nineteen year-old college student at Yale and [do] modeling work on the side, they're probably forty-five years old and live in the basement of their parents' house. And they're probably an online predator. It's a reality."

Sometimes the press write stories about Taylor that aren't true. When the Brazilian news network Globo published a piece claiming that a source had told them that Taylor's mom had banned her from performing there because it was a "third world country," fans around the world were stunned. Taylor's representatives quickly put the matter straight, telling BuzzFeed: "There is absolutely no truth" to the report. In fact, Andrea was born in Venezuela and Taylor's grandmother had hosted a TV show in Puerto Rico, so to claim that she was anti Latin America was just ridiculous.

Taylor would love to visit Brazil again if her schedule allows her to do so—she's just so busy, she hasn't had a chance yet.

DID YOU KNOW?

Taylor's song "Mean" from her third album, *Speak Now*, is her response to the comments people made about her singing off-key during her Grammy performance in 2010 and her experiences of being bullied at school. She revealed to the Associated Press in November 2011: "It's a song I wrote on a really, really bad day, but it has produced so many happy days for me since." She told NPR: "To stand up at the Grammys two years later, to sing that song and get a standing ovation for it, and to win two Grammys for that particular song, I think was the most gratifying experience I've ever had in my life."

Cláudia is twenty and from Jundiaí, São Paulo. Her favorite songs are "You Belong With Me," "Blank Space" and "Invisible." She says: "I became a Swiftie when I was thirteen. 'You Belong With Me' was the first song of Tay's that I listened to, so it's always going to be special to me. I love 'Blank Space'—the lyrics are brilliant and I love the music video. It's a song that shows how strong Taylor is and that she's not a naïve woman. The video was at the start of Taylor's new era. Tay's songs are so relatable and 'Invisible' is the perfect song to listen to when you're feeling a bit sad because it picks you right up.

"I can't choose just one thing I love about Taylor. I love everything about her. She is so strong, she's a talented songwriter, she has an amazing smile, she genuinely cares about her fans and she has an incredible voice. She's one of a kind and she's someone I really look up to.

DID YOU KNOW?

"Blank Space" from her fifth album, *1989*, won Taylor two MTV Video Music Awards in 2015—Best Pop Video and Best Female Video.

"Taylor doesn't visit Brazil very often but when she does, it makes me so happy. I love being a Swiftie and will always support Taylor in whatever she does in the future."

CHAPTER 7

CANADA

Canadian Swifties have lots of opportunities to see Taylor, as she spends quite a lot of time in their country when touring. Taylor is so thankful for their support and told Digital Spy: "I just feel so proud that my fans are always nice to other fans. They don't say hateful things. They don't say they're going to set people on fire or anything. They're not sending death threats to other people."

On July 6, 2015, she tweeted: "Back on the road! Insane crowd in Ottawa tonight! #1989TourOttawa" along with a photograph of herself standing onstage, her arm in the air, with thousands of lights from her fans' phones. That night she'd told the Swifties in the audience: "I love Canada. Canada is so cool!"

DID YOU KNOW?

Taylor wrote her song "The Outside" from her first album, *Taylor Swift*, when she was twelve. She explained to *Entertainment Weekly*: "I wrote that about the scariest feeling I've ever felt: going to school, walking down the hall, looking at those faces and not knowing who you're gonna talk to that day."

During her 1989 tour dates in Canada, Taylor was supported by Canadian singer-songwriter Shawn Mendes. He would have loved to have invited Taylor to be his prom date but he figured she was "past those days." Shawn told ET Canada: "Touring with her is actually really amazing. It's really awesome. She's just so kind and she's always hanging out."

When Taylor performed at the Rexall Place in Alberta, Canada, on August 4, she had a horrible shock when a man in the audience lunged onto the stage and grabbed her ankle during her performance of "Bad Blood." It all happened so fast, but thankfully her security team stepped in and prevented her from coming to any harm. But she didn't let the incident interrupt the show and carried on with the performance like a true professional.

DID YOU KNOW?

Taylor came up with the melody for "Long Live" when she was in her dressing room, waiting for the encore at one of her shows. It was a song she would dedicate to all the people she works with.

For first night in Toronto, she welcomed country singer Keith Urban on to the stage and together they sang Keith's hits, "John Cougar," "John Deere," "John 3:16" and "Somebody Like You." On her second night in the city, she sang "Boom Clap" with British singer-songwriter Charli XCX.

In Vancouver she invited the Norwegian singing and songwriting duo Nico and Vinz to perform their song, "Am I Wrong." Afterward, she shared a photo on Twitter of herself and the boys with the message: "I am OBSESSED with @ nicoandvinz and so was that Vancouver stadium crowd!! They are absolutely dynamic performers, the most down to earth guys, and "Am I Wrong" is such a brilliant song. SO HAPPY TONIGHT and so in awe of great artists like this."

Australian singer-songwriter Vance Joy was Taylor's supporting act for the majority of the 1989 shows and Canadian Swifties loved him. Vance told *Billboard*: "She's so lovely and told me she's excited to have me on tour. I try to communicate how grateful I feel to get this opportunity. And I always make sure I thank her when I'm onstage, just because it's a pleasure to be on this tour."

DID YOU KNOW?

Taylor wrote "Out Of The Woods" from her fifth album, *1989*, about One Direction's Harry Styles.

Sofia is fifteen and from Surrey, British Columbia. Her favorite songs are "New Romantics," "Sparks Fly" and "Red." Her favorite music video is *Shake It Off*. She says: "It's such a fun video and whenever I watch it, I always feel like dancing and it makes me happy. What I love about Taylor the most is just her. When I went to her 1989 concert in Vancouver she was so nice, and even though I was sitting on the balcony, I felt like I already had met her . . . like I was visiting an old friend from a long time ago. Being a fan in Canada is pretty normal. Once in a while I'll tweet Taylor, hoping she will reply, but then I realize that a million other people are doing the same thing at the exact same time.

"My cousin and I took part in a flash mob in Vancouver to try to win backstage passes to meet her. We didn't end up winning but we had a blast dancing to 'Shake It Off' with a bunch of other Swifties! Since we didn't win, we bought a bouquet of kale because we know Taylor loves kale. We thought that maybe by carrying the bouquet around at the concert her mom would see us and take us to meet Taylor, but security wouldn't let us take the bouquet in, which was a real shame. We left it at the customer services desk and they said she would get it, but I guess I'll never know unless I meet her someday!"

Fahey is thirteen and from Quebec City. Her favorite three songs are "Mine," "Blank Space" and "Bad Blood." She says: "I love how Taylor is always here for her fans, supporting them and doing everything she can for them. Being a Swiftie in Canada can be lonely at times because there aren't lots of Swiftie events to go to, but we support Taylor whenever we can.

"I've only been a Swiftie for a relatively short space of time but I know I'll be a fan of Taylor's forever. My favorite music video Taylor has done is *We Are Never Ever Getting Back Together*, but each video she makes is great. Every time she wins an award I feel so lucky that I've picked her to be my hero and my inspiration and I'm so, so proud of her for being the amazing person she is."Sarah is twenty-five and from Toronto. Her favorite three songs are "Long Live," "The Other Side Of The Door'" and "I Wish You Would." Her favorite music video is *Our Song*. She says: "I love that Taylor cares so much about her fans and she does everything she can to interact with us as much as she can. I love how she doesn't care what people think of her and she's always true to herself. She's gotten me through some tough times in my life and I can relate to her.

"Being a Canadian Swiftie is fantastic, although it sucks sometimes that we don't get nearly as much merchandise as the States do or nearly as many appearances. But I'm still grateful because Taylor doesn't get to visit every country, so we're lucky we get to see her as much as we do.

"I'm a dedicated Swiftie and when Taylor was going to be appearing on the Much Music channel in 2010, I decided to wait outside in the cold for eight hours to see if I could catch a glimpse of her. I'm only small and got pushed out of the way when she arrived, which was disappointing because I couldn't get a photo taken with her or ask for an autograph.

"Two years later, I managed to see Taylor at her *Red* album release, at Much Music. I had made a video explaining why I was such a huge fan and had submitted it to the music channel. They really liked it and had invited me to come into the studio to see Taylor. Taylor was amazing as usual, and at the end of the event I was given a sample bottle of her perfume. It was a fun day.

"Seeing Taylor perform live is incredible—I went to her Speak Now Tour and it was the most magical concert I've ever been to. She put so much thought into the tour and I was blown away with her stage presence. I also loved that she covered some Canadian artists like Avril Lavigne and Justin Bieber. She isn't afraid to tailor her performance depending on which country she's in—something that not many other artists do.

"I also went to Taylor's Red Tour and it was such a fun concert. Me and my friend Jessica jammed out so hard and lost our voices in the process. Taylor cut her knee unfortunately, but the show went on because she didn't want to let anyone down.

"I was lucky enough to see her 1989 show twice, and both nights were amazing in their own ways. She really puts on a great show. I loved her little remakes of certain songs like 'Love Story' and 'I Knew You Were Trouble.' For the shows I went to see, the special guests were Keith Urban and Charli XCX, and they were great. And the opening acts were fantastic too and really got us excited to see Taylor.

"I can't wait to see what Taylor does next; every album she does is amazing. She's going to keep making music for a long time and I'm going to be supporting her every step of the way."

Brooke is fifteen and from Regina, Saskatchewan. Her favorite songs are "Wildest Dreams," "Bad Blood" and "Stay Stay Stay." She says: "Everything about Tay is flawless, of course, but if I had to choose one thing that I love about her the most I'd say her personality, she's so generous and caring.

"I don't know of any Swifties that live in my home city, which is a real shame because I'd love to meet up to talk about Tay and her music. Tay is so busy touring the world that she can't spend too long in any one country, but when she visits Canada, we try to show her as much support as we can. Tay might not know me on a personal level but I'll always be a Swiftie.

"She is an amazing artist and I get excited every time she releases a new song and music video. My favorite video currently is *Blank Space* because it's so fun and suits the song so well. My favorite album is *1989*, but this often changes depending on what I'm going through at the time. I love the photos she puts up on Twitter and when she tells us something funny her cats have done.

"I love going to see her in concert and I enjoy watching her performances and interviews online. My favorite performance has to be when she performed at the Jingle Bell Ball in 2014 on her twenty-fifth birthday. She sang 'I Knew You Were Trouble' and 'Shake It Off.' The crowd went wild."

Natasha is twenty-two and from Abbotsford, British Columbia. Her favorite three songs are "All Too Well," "Wildest Dreams" and "The Moment I Knew." She says: "My favorite music video has to be *Blank Space*. The costumes, the location, and everything about it is beautiful, enchanting and completely flawless, including the story behind the song, that 'You are not your mistakes and you are not the opinion of someone who doesn't know you.' Taylor makes all her music videos have a powerful message.

"My favorite performance Taylor has done is 'All Too Well' at the Grammys in 2014. It's my favorite song from the *Red* album and she sang it from many requests from her fans—that's what I love about her: she listens to what her fans want.

"I became a fan in 2006 when I was thirteen. My sister went to see Rascal Flatts in Vancouver and Taylor was there, opening for them. When my sister got home, she told me I had to listen to her songs, that she was an amazing performer and I would love her music. That's how I became a fan. After that day, I have admired her as a role model, singer, fashion icon and songwriter.

"As much as I love all the albums, my favorite is *1989*. I feel like I can relate to every song on it, about being in your twenties and all the adventures, love and friendships you have in those times. Every song on that album I feel connected to and get a strong emotion or feeling that helps me get through hard times and that makes my day brighter.

"There are so many reasons why I love Taylor. I think it's amazing that she writes all her own music, that it's so lyrically beautiful in a way that connects emotionally with millions of people. Her performances are always so breathtaking, different and inspiring. Taylor's music is just part of why I love her so much. She made me feel like it was okay if your mom was your best friend growing up, that being nice to people was the most important (which I already thought). But at that time, those things were not cool. She made being nice, being who you are and treating people kindly a cool thing. That's why I love her so much. I love that she is close with her family. I love how she treats her fans like friends and does surprises for them (Secret Sessions, T-party, Club Red and Loft 89, etc.). All of her meet and greets are for free. She is such a selfless, inspiring, admirable human being. Taylor has been the top charitable celebrity for years. She constantly finds ways to improve her music, her performances and, mostly, the lives of others. I hope that she reads this and that one day I get the chance to thank her for everything she has done for me and tell her how much I love her—'People haven't always been there for me, but music has.' I love you, Taylor.

"I'm so grateful to have been to three of Taylor's concerts. The first time I saw her was the Speak Now concert. It was very theatrical and had amazing costumes. It was like the whole concert was a story that she was singing and going through the scenes. Red Tour was amazing in a different way. For me it was more emotional than Speak Now. She did many speeches before the songs and she would usually play one song of an artist from the city she was in. The 1989 Tour was a big change in comparison, since it is a pop album. She had more dancers. It felt like more lights, confetti and fireworks.

"1989 is a great mix of all her concerts. She brought out a special guest at almost every show, including when I saw her! Her speeches make me cry, she never fails with surprises and her presence onstage is so powerful. Taylor performs each song so intensely that you feel like you were there when she was going through something. In 1989, she would play one of her old songs from her old albums, and in Vancouver she played 'Sparks Fly'—that was my favorite part of the concert because it was unexpected and it's my favorite song from that album. People of all ages are at her concerts, which I find is also very cool. It is definitely something you want to experience."

CHAPTER 8
CHILE

Taylor might never have visited Chile, but this hasn't stopped her from gaining thousands of fans there. If you're a Swiftie living in Chile then you should join the Taylor Swift Chile fan page on Facebook. There are over 75,000 fans of the page and they hold regular Swiftie parties, events and competitions.

Choosing a favorite album or song is difficult for any fan, and Chilean fans will often debate which is the best when they meet up. Taylor has written so many heartfelt songs about experiences she and her friends have gone through. She found writing "Tied Together With a Smile" from her first album difficult to write because it was about a friend of hers who was bulimic. The message Taylor wanted to put across in the song was that no matter what her friends go through, she's always going to be there to support them.

Many fans enjoy decoding Taylor's songs and particularly like the Jake Gyllenhaal-inspired ones. In "State Of Grace" from her fourth album *Red*, Taylor mentions that the lovers have "twin fire signs" and "four blue eyes"—both Taylor and Jake have blue eyes and they're both Sagittarians. In "All Too Well" she mentions the scarf that she wore throughout their relationship, and autumn, which was the time when she visited the home of Jake's sister, Maggie. "We Are Never Ever Getting Back Together," "Red" and "Sad Beautiful Tragic" are also believed to be songs about Jake. Taylor wrote her single "Red" because "some things are just hard to forget because the emotions involved with them were so intense and to me, intense emotion is red," she explained to the hosts of *Good Morning America*.

DID YOU KNOW?

Many Swifties believe that Taylor was inspired to write "Style" from her *1989* album after she dated Harry Styles from One Direction.

Jake Gyllenhaal didn't actually mind Taylor using their relationship for her album, *Red*, and told her that listening to the album was bittersweet for him because it was like looking through a photo album. Taylor much preferred this response to the one she got from another ex, who sent her angry emails when he heard the tracks she'd written about him. Many fans believe this ex to be John Mayer.

Fefy is twenty-one and from Concepción. She says: "It's really difficult to pick my three favorite songs. I would say 'Tim

McGraw' because it was the first song of Taylor's that I heard. I was only thirteen and the first chords of that song literally saved my life. 'Long Live' is really special to me because it's like an anthem for me and my best friend. We've been best friends for thirteen years and we've been through a lot. I was bullied and she was the only person who was next to me, fighting against all those 'dragons.' My third favorite song has to be 'New Romantics.' I've been listening to Taylor's music for the past eight years, and all through my teens I felt she was writing about my life, and this song is how I feel nowadays. I love the line, 'Heartbreak is the National Anthem we sing it proudly.'

"My favorite music video is, of course, *Shake It Off*. It was the beginning of a new era and in the video we can see this brand new Taylor Swift being herself, no matter what people say! Totally fearless, totally happy, totally comfortable with herself . . . and that's everything!"What I love the most about Taylor is the way she lives her life. I mean, she's a huge celebrity, she could be a total diva, but she is the opposite of that. She's kind, she's nice with her fans, with her crew, with her family and friends, and she fights for what she believes. She's the best role model I could ever ask for.

"Being a Swiftie in Chile isn't easy but I'll never give up. Taylor's never been here, but I hope she will one day. Brazil is the closest place she has been to. The only way to get merchandise is to buy it on the Internet and it's very expensive. It was only last year that Keds began to be sold here. And, of course, we're never part of the tours. But to be honest, I never lose faith. I've had the same 'Taylor Swift Concert' jar to save money in for the last eight years. I know, for sure, that she'll come to Chile someday."

CHAPTER 9

CZECH REPUBLIC

Taylor hasn't visited the Czech Republic and her early albums weren't played on the radio there. However, when she released *1989*, her music started to be played and she now has a small group of devoted Swifties who try to promote her as much as they can.

They run a group on Facebook called Taylor Swift (Czech Republic), which has more than six hundred fans, and they post the latest news on Taylor. Whenever a fan goes to see Taylor in concert in another country, they make sure they take as many videos and photos as possible so they can share them with other Czech fans.

Czech Swifties launched a petition to try and encourage Taylor to bring her 1989 show to their country, but sadly they didn't receive many signatures.

DID YOU KNOW?

"Should've Said No" was the last song Taylor wrote for her debut album, *Taylor Swift*. It only took twenty minutes to write and then she went ahead and recorded it pretty much straight away. It was about a boy called Sam who had cheated on her and the message is about saying no to temptation. When the song came out, the boy concerned got very nervous and texted Taylor to ask her not to draw attention to him in interviews. Taylor told *Women's Health*: "All I could think was, well, you should've said no. That's what the song is about."

Gabriela Daníčková wrote on the petition page: "I'm signing this because I really want to go to her concert and see her perform live but I'm afraid that it's too far away for me."

Tatiana Balážiková added: "I would like to see a Taylor Swift concert in the Czech Republic. It would be awesome for all the fans from our country to see her here."

Even though there aren't currently many Czech Swifties, Taylor's music is growing in popularity there so hopefully in the future she will come and visit—even if it's just for a day.

Denisa is eighteen and from Prague. Her favorite three songs are "Clean," "Back To December" and "New Romantics." She says: "I first heard Taylor's music when I was eleven and it completely changed my life. I'd always loved singing, but once I became a Swiftie it became my big passion. I would love to be a professional singer one day.

"Taylor inspired me to start playing guitar when I was twelve, she encouraged me to start writing my own music, and she's taught me to never give up on my dream. She's taught me so much through her music. I know that without her influence, I would be a completely different person. She's so kind and I never feel alone when I have her music.

"The sad thing is that I've never met another Czech Swiftie. In my country, people do sometimes know Taylor, but mainly because of her last album. They haven't followed her for as long as I have. I really wish Taylor would visit here sometime, it would mean so much to me. I traveled to Germany to see her perform her Red show but I couldn't afford to go back for her 1989 Tour. I would love to see her perform live again; it would mean the world to me."

CHAPTER 10
FRANCE

Taylor always has a great time whenever she visits France. She didn't bring her Fearless Tour to the country but she did bring her Speak Now World Tour, performing at the Zénith de Paris. Many French Swifties traveled to the UK and Germany to watch her Red show in February 2014 and her 1989 show in June 2015 because she didn't have any dates in France and they didn't want to miss out.

When Taylor was in France for the NRJ Music Awards in January 2013 she performed her hit "We Are Never Ever Getting Back Together," and she changed some of the lyrics so she was speaking in French. Afterward, the host spoke to her in French and Taylor told him she was having a great time and that she loved France. She did really well speaking in French, even if it was only a few words.

DID YOU KNOW?

The inspiration for "Mary's Song (Oh My My My)" came from Taylor's neighbors, who came for dinner and told the Swifts how they fell in love. Taylor explained: "I thought it was so sweet, because you can go to the grocery store and read the tabloids, and see who's breaking up and cheating on each other—or just listen to some of my songs, ha-ha. But it was really comforting to know that all I had to do was go home and look next door to see a perfect example of forever."

On October 5, 2014, Taylor left New York to fly to France to promote her *1989* album. She was feeling pretty tired as she had to get up early to be at the airport and so shared a photo on Twitter of her feeling sorry for herself, wrapped in a quilt with a hot drink. She added the message: "bright eyed and ready to take on the next adventure! . . . . nope."

But Taylor didn't seem at all tired the next day when she was interviewed by various French TV show hosts and journalists. She made sure she spent time signing autographs and posed for photos with Swifties who had stood outside in the freezing cold to see her. During her interview on NRJ, she talked about the female singers who'd inspired her when she was growing up and how she was happy with two cats and wouldn't be getting a third anytime soon.

She'd brought some homemade cookies for the NRJ team to munch on during the interview, which was a nice touch, and answered all the questions from fans that were put to her. One fan wanted to know why she'd ditched guitars for automated drums and layered vocals in her new album. Taylor revealed: "I just felt myself naturally gravitating towards making pop music."

Another fan admitted that his friends make fun of him for listening to her music and call him gay. She responded by saying: "Listening to my music is just as manly as growing out a full beard. It's just like chopping up trees in the backyard and building a log cabin. Everyone knows that. You tell them that."

After the interview wrapped, Taylor had to perform "Shake It Off" on the talk show, *Le Grand Journal*, before she could head back to her hotel. As she traveled in the car that had been provided for her, she spotted the Eiffel Tower and took a photo to show her fans around the world. It wasn't the clearest picture in the world because it was raining heavily, but Taylor didn't mind, she was worn out.

If you're a French Swiftie, make sure you like the Taylor Swift France Facebook page. Currently, it has more than 109,000 fans and is a great place to find out about Swiftie events being run in your local area.

DID YOU KNOW?

Taylor worked with Dan Wilson, the former lead singer of the alternative rock band Semisonic and the man who cowrote Adele's hit "Someone Like You," on the writing of "Treacherous" for her fourth album. She had already figured out the melody and knew that she wanted the song to be about treachery but looked to Dan for more inspiration. They worked on it together and after they thought they'd finished the track, they suddenly decided to make the chorus rockier.

Julien is twenty and from Clermont-Ferrand. His favorite three songs are “Shake It Off,” “Tim McGraw” and “Last Kiss.” He met Taylor in March 2013 when she did a showcase in Paris for some of her biggest fans. She sang six songs acoustically and everyone watching was completely blown away. To see her performance for yourself, search for “Live on the Seine” on YouTube.

Julien almost didn’t get the chance to see the show because he’d failed to win tickets in the competition that radio station NRJ were running. He didn’t want to give up, though, and managed to find someone from Paris on Twitter who had won tickets but couldn’t make the show. He traveled for an hour and a half to meet the girl and get the tickets so he could meet Taylor.

During the intimate show, French Swifties got to ask Taylor questions. One fan wanted to know: “Do you prefer playing in stadiums or in intimate places like tonight?” Taylor replied: “I just love playing music. And I like playing in small venues. I’ll play on a boat, I’ll play on a plane, I’ll play anywhere; I’ll play on a stadium . . . It’s like, you know, I just love to play music and it’s fun to get to tell you the stories behind them, and we can do that more because there’s just a few of us here.”

After she had performed “I Knew You Were Trouble,” Julien asked her: “You play guitar, piano and ukulele, would you like to learn another instrument, maybe the drums?” Taylor replied: “Not really! It’s a horrible answer, but I like the instruments you can accompany yourself with—that you can play along. So, you know, I like guitar, banjo, ukulele, piano

. . . I think I would just rather focus on the instruments I play and continue to get better at playing the instruments I play."

Taylor was really touched when Julien said he liked the koa guitar that she was playing, commenting, "It's a wood that comes from Hawaii and I just became obsessed with this type of guitar when I was, like, twelve years old. I'm glad you like it."

Julien says: "During the concert Taylor was always looking at me, I guess because I was a guy and she might have thought I was handsome (or so I hope, lol). After she'd sung 'I Knew You Were Trouble,' she said that I knew all the words and asked me if I was American.

"I've also met her stylist, Joseph Cassell, twice, once in Paris, near Taylor's hotel and the second time on the boat, where we talked. Kamilah (her backing singer) was sweet. After the concert, we took a picture with Taylor. It was a group picture, ten fans at a time. When it was my turn, she recognized me and said something like 'Aww' and then she hugged me. It felt amazing. I didn't have the chance to talk to her properly because there wasn't much time.

"I loved having the opportunity to meet Taylor and I hope to meet her again soon. Being a fan in France is hard because she doesn't come here very often and she wasn't very well known here until *1989* started being played on the radio. I was really disappointed when her Red Tour didn't come here and that there were no *1989* tour dates either.

"I consider myself an active Swiftie because I love organizing Swiftie events. I organized a *1989* party, which was a huge success. It took place in Paris and we had several

Above: Taylor's family have always been incredibly supportive of her dreams, and she is as close to her parents Scott and Andrea (*left*) and brother Austin (*right*) as she has always been. *© Getty Images*

Below: Fans will do anything to get tickets to Taylor's concerts, and she knows how to put on a great show. *© Getty Images*

Above: No matter where Taylor goes in the world now she is greeted by huge crowds of fans, like here in China in 2014.

Below: Taylor always spots fans that she knows in the crowd, even if she's only met them once and when that crowd fills a stadium of over 65,000 people.

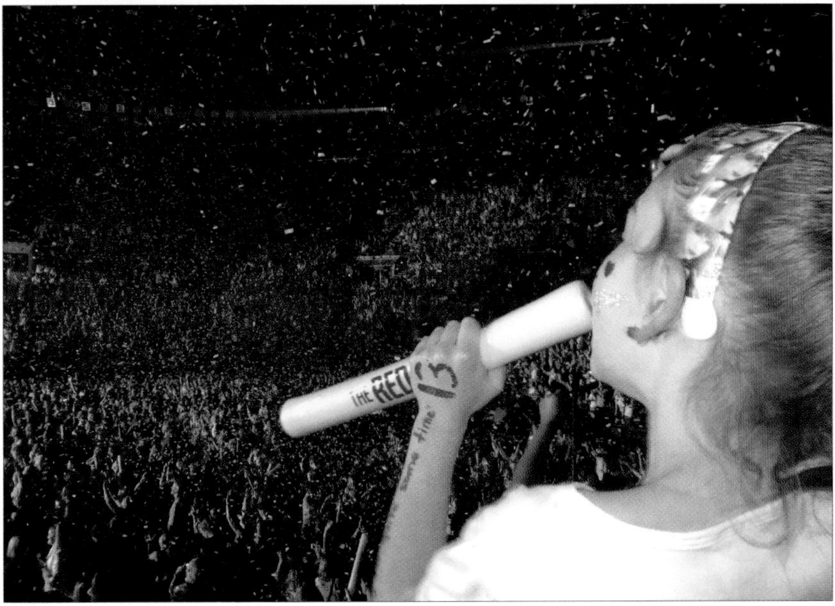

Above left: Taylor's fans come out in their thousands no matter where she goes, and they make signs, pictures, banners and everything else imaginable for Taylor to enjoy. *© Getty Images*

Above right: Taylor always finds time to take selfies with her biggest fans. *© Getty Images*

Below: Mia, 'New Zealand's number one Swiftie', sings along with Taylor on her Red tour.

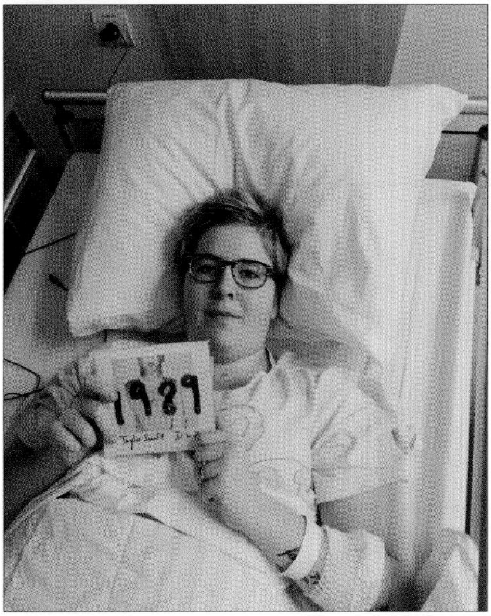

Above left: Sofia (*second from left*) with friends outside a Taylor concert in Canada.

Above right: Chloe from Southampton had her dreams come true when she met Taylor at a Secret Session.

Below left: Taylor met Demi, who was sadly diagnosed with Friedreich's Ataxia and so has to spend a lot of time in hospital, through the fantastic Make-a-Wish Foundation.

Below right: Jaime and her friends spent weeks making their costumes – but it was all worth it when they were chosen to meet Taylor.

activities for fans to enjoy, including a party listening to the album in a bar.

"I've been contacted by Taylor's staff by email because I'm such a big fan and hopefully next time there's another private event in France I'll be invited to come along. I'll never give up hope that I'll meet Taylor again."

CHAPTER 11

GERMANY

German Swifties feel very blessed to have had Taylor perform her concerts in their country. Although she didn't visit with Fearless, she performed her Speak Now World Tour show on March 12, 2011 in Oberhausen at the König-Pilsener Arena, her Red World show on February 7, 2014 in Berlin at O2 World, and her 1989 World Tour in Cologne at the Lanxess Arena on June 19 and 20, 2015.

Taylor might not be a linguist but she always tries to speak the native language of her fans, if she can. When she performed in Cologne she did her best, thanking fans, telling them it was cool that they had come to see her, asking how they were. Everyone screamed when she said: "I love Germany, I love Cologne, I love you."

DID YOU KNOW?

Taylor wrote her track "Our Song" when she was a student at Henderson High and she realized that she and her boyfriend didn't have a song. Rather than choose one from the charts at the time, she decide to write one herself by sitting down with her guitar and trying to figure out what she wanted to say.

Taylor wanted every night of her tour to be different. Backstage in Cologne, she told journalist Dan Wootton: "There's dancing, but it's not synchronized. I want to have space as a performer to change things every night.

"I have to be self-aware enough to know that a huge amount of expectation is put on me. It doesn't look like any of my other tours, it doesn't feel like any of my other tours, that's something I'm very proud of."

If you're a German Swiftie why not check out the Taylor Swift Germany page of Facebook? The fans who run the page are constantly adding new photos of Taylor and sharing the latest news articles on her. Currently, the page has nearly 600,000 likes.

DID YOU KNOW?

Taylor finds inspiration for songs everywhere. After seeing a photo of Ethel and Robert F. Kennedy having fun at a ball in the 1940s, she wrote "Starlight" for her fourth album, *Red*.

Lilly is twenty years old and comes from Frankfurt. Her favorite songs are "Crazier," "Mean" and "Come In With The Rain." She says: "I like Taylor because her songs are so honest that I feel like she's not lying in them to get attention. She really helped me to get through school—I didn't really have friends, at least none I could really trust. Thanks to Taylor, I was able to make some good friends with fans from across Germany and wider afield, which was so nice.

"Being a Swiftie in Germany used to be rather hard, because Taylor wasn't very well known. My friends and I used to email radio stations and magazines to try to promote her music and encourage the radio stations to play her songs. I became friends with a UK Swiftie online, and when I moved to the UK to study it was nice to meet her in person. Being a Swiftie in the UK is much easier than being a Swiftie in Germany."

In 2012, Lilly managed to meet Taylor when the singer visited Frankfurt for the MTV Europe Music Awards. Lilly explains: "My friend and I decided to try and roam the city in the hope of finding her. We went there on the Saturday, but we weren't lucky—we couldn't find her or her entourage anywhere. We did meet two other Swifties, though, and decided to swap contact details, just in case.

"That night, one of the girls sent me a photo of the entrance of the hotel that Taylor was staying in—but she didn't have the name of the hotel or any more information. I forwarded the picture to my friend as she knows Frankfurt really well. She actually recognized the pattern of stones on the ground and knew what hotel it was! I told the other Swifties immediately, and we decided to meet there in the morning.

"I spent the night working on a little present for Taylor. I formed a little rose out of clay, painted it red and put glitter on top. The next morning, we went to Frankfurt really early and were the first people to arrive at the hotel. However, word got around and soon many more people arrived. Security had to put up fences to hold us back. And then we waited. At four o'clock in the afternoon I was fed up because it was a really cold November day and I hadn't eaten anything for hours. A tiny bit of me felt like giving up, but I'm so glad I didn't because Taylor suddenly appeared.

"I was so awestruck I wasn't able to take a photo with my camera. Taylor had walked past me before I realized what was happening. I wanted her to have the rose I had made for her so much that I called after her, 'Taylor! Please! I made this for you! I made it myself, please take it!'

"Taylor turned back, smiled, took the rose and said: 'Awww,' then she took the camera out of my hand and said, 'You wanna take a picture?'

"I don't remember if I said yes. I think I just gasped. She put her face next to mine, I felt her hair and smelled her perfume—she was wearing Wonderstruck Enchanted. I was so happy. So, so, happy! She took an amazing picture and then went on. My hands were shaking so much that I accidentally deleted the picture. But it was there.

"I don't know why Taylor chose me to take a picture with. She took only two or three pictures with fans that day. I'm just glad she got my present. I hope it made her day a little too.

Jessica is sixteen and from Berge, Sachsen-Anhalt. Her three favorite songs are "Haunted," "22" and "All You Had To Do Was Stay." She loves how friendly and down to earth Tay is. Jessica says: "My favorite music video is *Shake It Off* because it cheers me up and it has a great meaning. Also because she invited one hundred fans to be in the video, which I think is so sweet of her.

"I love being a German Swiftie, but being a Swiftie in Germany around the *Fearless* and *Speak Now* eras was kinda hard because country music isn't very popular in Germany. Whenever someone asked me which artist I liked the most and I replied Taylor Swift, most of them looked at me weird and asked who she was. Or if they had heard of her, they'd ask why I listen to this type of music.

"Back then, you never really heard of her in the news. The *Red* era was a bit better—more people began to like her because her music started to be more pop, and in general you heard and read more about her in the news. And now in the *1989* era I kinda feel like a lot more people are starting to like her and become Swifties. I think this is mainly due to her music being pop now, the most popular genre in Germany, and the fact that the media talk so much about her. She's constantly mentioned on German TV, newspapers and magazines.

"I've never met Tay, unfortunately, but I've been to see her in concert a couple times. They've been the best days of my life—a Taylor Swift concert is like a two-hour dance party with thousands of your friends. Who wouldn't love that?"

CHAPTER 12

HONG KONG

Taylor performed her Speak Now concert in Hong Kong on February 21, 2011 and it was a night that the Swifties in the audience will never forget.

In 2014, the Taylor Swift Hong Kong Fan Club created a wonderful video, encouraging Taylor to bring the 1989 World Tour to Hong Kong. They posted it on YouTube and underneath wrote further messages of encouragement for the singer.

Catherine Peng wrote: "pls pls pls come tay for 1989 world tour! i am literally begging on my knees. Waiting for u!!"

Alvin So Ching Yan added: "We miss Taylor Swift."

In the video they say: "Hong Kong wants Taylor Swift. Hello. We are Swifties from Hong Kong. Taylor was here in Hong Kong in 2011, back when she was having her Speak Now Tour. She didn't visit Hong Kong again in the Red Tour. We miss her a lot . . . We wonder if she remembers us . . .

whether she remembers how loud we had screamed that night? Or how well did we sing together?

"We Hong Kong Swifties made a fan project for Taylor! Hong Kong wants Taylor Swift! #hongkongwantstaylorswift."

Sadly, Taylor didn't bring her 1989 World Tour to Hong Kong, but hopefully she will visit again in the future. Hong Kong Swifties are very dedicated and regularly hold Swiftie events. One such event was held on July 26, 2014. They get together to talk about Taylor, sing songs and play games.

DID YOU KNOW?

The guy for whom Taylor wrote the "Hey Stephen" song from her second album, *Fearless*, was singer and guitarist Stephen Barker Liles of the band Love and Theft. They opened for Taylor back in 2008 and she developed a bit of a crush. She only let him know that she'd written the song when the album was about to be released. Stephen was thrilled and emailed her to say thanks. He later told *People* magazine what Taylor's like, as a friend: "We've become great friends since Love and Theft started opening shows for her. I think everyone would agree she's a total sweetheart and anyone would be lucky to go out with her."

He told Planet Verge: "Taylor genuinely loves people in a way only the Lord would."

Sandy is twenty-two and from Hong Kong. Her three favorite songs are "Fearless," "Everything Has Changed" and "Blank Space" (which is also her favorite music video). She says: "I became a Swiftie when I was fifteen. I was walking around a CD store with my mom and sis, and I saw Tay's *Fearless* album. I decided to give it a try. After using the earphones provided to listen to it, I was blown away by how amazing it was and bought it immediately!

"I love how sincere Taylor is, both to her friends and her Swifties. I feel really connected to other fans in Hong Kong and because there aren't many of us, we stick together. I really wanted to see her Speak Now show in 2011 when it came to Hong Kong but I couldn't because I had exams and school. Taylor Nation haven't held any fan events in Hong Kong, which is a really disappointing, but hopefully they will consider holding some here in the future.

"In June 2015 I traveled to New York with my family to see Taylor's 1989 show in Philadelphia on the 13th. It was the best night of my life! Seeing her perform 'New Romantics,' 'Blank Space,' 'How You Get The Girl' . . . it was incredible. Having the opportunity to see Taylor perform live is something I'll never forget and I feel so privileged.

"I would have loved to have been chosen for Loft 89 but, alas, it wasn't to be."

CHAPTER 13

HUNGARY

Taylor has never toured in Hungary and she doesn't have a large fan base there, so it can be tough for Swifties living in this country. Luckily, thanks to social media they can be part of the wider Swiftie community and see clips from her shows on YouTube.

If you live in Hungary, why not like the Facebook page Taylor Swift Hungary? Currently, there are just over 900 fans of the page, but more people are joining all the time.

Nora is seventeen and from Debrecen, on the eastern side of Hungary. She says: "I have always loved Taylor's music, but it wasn't until the summer of 2012 that I really started to listen to all her songs, not just her singles. I found her songs so relatable and catchy.

"Eventually I became a fan of hers, watching every available interview, concert video and basically anything that had something to do with her. I love so many of her tracks that it's difficult to choose only three favorite songs, but if I had to, I would say 'Mary's Song (Oh My My My),' 'Long Live' and 'Shake It Off.' My favorite music video has got to be the one for 'I'm Only Me When I'm With You.' It's so heartwarming and shows her love for her family, friends and fans.

"It's really hard to be a Swiftie in Hungary since she's (unfortunately) not very popular here, and it's so hard to buy any kind of merchandise. The fact that Taylor's official merchandise store doesn't ship to Hungary is really disappointing. Moreover, since I live in Central Europe, I can't go to concerts because she doesn't come here on tour, so I'm waiting for the 1989 Tour DVD to be released."

DID YOU KNOW?

Originally, Taylor was going to include "White Horse" on her third album, *Speak Now*, but after the producers of the hit show *Grey's Anatomy* asked if they could use it in an episode she decided to include it on *Fearless* instead. She confided to *Billboard*: "You should've seen the tears streaming down my face when I got the phone call that they were going to use that song. I have never been that excited. This is my life's goal, to have a song on *Grey's Anatomy*. My love of *Grey's Anatomy* has never wavered. It's my longest relationship to date!"

CHAPTER 14
INDIA

Another country where it's hard to be a Swiftie is India. Taylor has never visited, but fans are hopeful one day she might do so as she loves Indian food. She told ASOS: "I make a really good Indian roasted cauliflower for my vegetarian friends, which they request when they come over. I roast the cauliflower in olive oil and add a yogurt sauce with spices and pine nuts."

She also shared with the *Times of India* back in November 2012: "I haven't planned anything yet, but I would love to come down and perform, or even just come for a visit.

"I have heard a lot about the Taj Mahal, Kashmir, Delhi and South India. I like historic monuments. They depict so much about a particular culture. I am a travel junkie who loves to explore a lot of local food and style. I would love to taste some great Indian food. I would love to sing for a Bollywood movie. I am open to offers and learning a few Hindi words."

Sadly, Taylor has been so busy over the past few years that she hasn't had the chance to visit India, but hopefully next time she gets an extended break she'll think of making a trip there—her Indian Swifties would love to meet her.

Pria is fifteen and from Mumbai. She became a fan in 2011 after her best friend ditched her and she was feeling really hurt and upset. Hearing "The Story Of Us" really helped her get through this stressful time because everything Taylor was singing about she could relate to. She admits: "I felt like I could share my loneliness with someone. I felt like Taylor could speak for me when I had no voice, that I could tell her things that I'm most afraid to share. She became my inspiration.

"Today, there are literally so many things that I love about Taylor, but if I had to choose one it'd be her dedication to everything. Her goals, career, people! She is dedicated to achieving her goals, she goes out of her way to express her gratitude to people and she's so humble.

"Out of all her songs I love 'Fearless' the most—this song inspires me to be brave and it's a song that helped me bond with my mom. 'Mine' is also a special song to me because it helps me when I'm feeling down. It reminds me that there might be no happily ever afters but there are moments that are just as good as a fairytale ending, memories that I'll think of when I'm old.

"My favorite video is *I Knew You Were Trouble*. It's so well acted, it's like a mini movie. Taylor is brilliant in it—when she's screaming for the men to stop fighting, it seems so real.

"Being a Swiftie in India is really hard. Most good websites don't ship merchandise here and the ones that do either have really ugly stuff or are really expensive. Being a fan of any artist is hard here because no one ever tours unless they're DJs or EDM [electronic dance music] artists. Ed Sheeran did come here to perform, but I had exams at school so couldn't make his show.

"Will I meet Taylor face to face one day? I really hope so."

CHAPTER 15

INDONESIA

Taylor made a big impression on her Indonesian Swifties when she brought her Red Tour to the MEIS Ancol in Jakarta on June 4, 2014. She performed to over 8,000 Swifties and her supporting act was Nicole Zefanya. A huge Swiftie herself, Nicole had to win a competition called "Ride to Fame" in order to be chosen as Taylor's opening act. She was so happy when she found out she was the winner and couldn't wait to tell her friends at school. To perform on the same stage as Taylor was a dream come true!

Taylor told *Get Scoop* magazine at the time why she simply had to visit Indonesia. She admitted: "Well, since two years ago, Indonesia has been on my priority list. But since there was a scheduling issue, I have only been able to hold a concert here now. Because my fans here kept continuously sending me their tweets, I made up my mind I must go there this year!

"I chose uncommon countries to visit because I just wanted to experience something new. Early on, I was not very confident in facing the challenge of concerts in these locations, but presented with the reality that all tickets to these concerts sold out, I could only think. 'How could such countries that I have never visited before be this excited?'

"I don't know why my music is so popular in Asia but I feel really flattered since English is not their mother tongue. They really tried to learn from my songs, and to sing them while I'm onstage. So I feel so proud to be able to have such a great influence on them."

DID YOU KNOW?

Taylor got the inspiration for her track "You Belong With Me" from her second album, *Fearless*, when she was traveling on her tour bus. She explained to *Self* how she heard a member of her band telling his girlfriend over the phone: "Baby, of course I love you more than music, I'm sorry. I had to go to soundcheck. I'm so sorry I didn't stay on the phone."

She decided to write a song about how the guy should realize that he has more in common with her in her "T-shirts" rather than his girlfriend, who wears "short skirts."

The Taylor Swift Indonesia Facebook page has more than 31,000 fans and is a great place for Indonesian fans to discuss why they love Taylor so much. If you're from Indonesia, you definitely should join.

Devy is nineteen and one of Taylor's biggest Indonesian fans. She has supported the singer from the beginning, ever since she saw an article about Tay in her big sister's magazine and listened to "Love Story" for the first time. Devy loves all of Tay's songs but she's especially fond of "All Too Well," "The Way I Loved You" and "Treacherous."

She says: "I don't know why I love her. I guess it's because she's such a sweet person, smart and beautiful inside and out. She's a strong person and she's been through a lot. So many people make fun of her but it doesn't stop her, it encourages her. Being a Swiftie in Indonesia means that you can't always get her merchandise because Taylor's web store doesn't ship worldwide. There are stores here that sell merchandise, but it's so overpriced because of the shipping fee that I can't afford it. I only have her CDs and other little things, but not a T-shirt or blanket or bags.

"Taylor came to Indonesia, bringing her Red Tour, and it was fantastic. I got to touch her hands several times during the concert but we didn't have Club Red, which was a shame. A few days before the concert, Indonesia's biggest official fansite for Taylor (@swiftindonesia) organized a national Swiftie gathering and it also had a *1989* album launch event. I went to both events. At the *1989* album launch event, we were asked to wear a costume and I decided to dress up as the Statue of Liberty. I won the best costume prize, which was a pair of Black Sneaky Cat Keds, which were the most wanted shoes for Swifties at that time. At that event, one of the admins from @swiftindonesia asked me to join them, so I now help provide the latest news for Swifties in Indonesia, as well as studying engineering at university."

Rara is twenty and from Jakarta. She loves being an Indonesian Swiftie and meeting other fans on Twitter or in person. Her favorite three songs are "All Too Well," "Story Of Us" and "I Know Places." She says: "I love Taylor because she's a wonderful role model. She's taught me to be kind to everyone I meet and not to take friendships or life for granted. She encourages me to laugh at myself, make mistakes, and give back to those who have given so much to me.

"If I had the opportunity to meet Taylor one day, I'd thank her. I'd say, 'Thank you, Taylor, for reminding me how much I can do every day to show people I care for them. You've show me how just taking the time to send a positive comment can help turn someone's day around.'

"Just reading the tweets that Taylor sends each day puts a smile on my face. I especially like her tweets about her cats. When she tweeted a photo of her leg with a massive scratch in March 2015, with the message 'Great work, Meredith, I was just trying to love you and now you owe me 40 million dollars,' it was so funny because the press had been talking about how Taylor had insured her legs for millions of dollars just a few days earlier."

Other top cat-related tweets:

"Watching tv with my cat while eating Toy Story fruit snacks. So basically I'm 80 and 5 at the same time."

"In Vancouver—just realized you guys got my Twitter up to 30 million followers?!?! So cool considering I only tweet about my cat and food."

"That moment when your cat casually walks up, then abruptly ATTACKS your custom satin Oscar de la Renta gown during your fitting for Met Ball."

CHAPTER 16
IRELAND

Ireland sure loves Taylor and every time she's due to visit their country, Irish Swifties get super excited. She didn't tour Ireland with Fearless, but she performed her Speak Now Tour in Dublin at the 3Arena on March 27, 2011. Irish Swifties were disappointed when the Red Tour didn't come to Ireland, but many fans decided to hop across to the UK to see one of her shows there instead so they didn't miss out. Taylor made it up to her Irish fans by announcing she'd be playing not one but two dates in Ireland as part of her 1989 World Tour. She performed to audiences of over 25,000 on June 29 and 30, 2015.

When Taylor's traveling the world she does miss her friends, whether that's her school friends, Britany and Abigail, or celebrity friends like Selena Gomez and the Haim sisters. She confessed to Mark Sutherland from the Independent.ie: "The thing about my girlfriends right now is that none of them needs me for anything other than friendship. I love the fact that they are all passionate about their jobs, whatever their jobs are. A lot of celebrity-type people have this group of people around them, where their friends' main priority is them, and they feel comfortable with that dynamic. I don't feel comfortable with that dynamic."

While promoting her *1989* album in London in October 2014, Taylor flew some Irish journalists there so they could have the opportunity to interview her about her new music. One of the journalists was Rachael Ryan from Spin 1038's breakfast show, *Fully Charged*.

In her one-on-one time with Taylor, Rachael tried to get her to say some things in Irish for her Irish fans, and although Taylor played along to begin with, she stopped. She thought Rachael was trying to trick her into saying something rude when she asked her to say *Conas atá tú*, which means "How are you?" Taylor shook her head when Rachael said: "You're not going to say it, are you?" To which Taylor replied: "No, because I think it means something like sex."

DID YOU KNOW?

For her second album, *Fearless*, Taylor decided to duet with singer-songwriter Colbie Caillat on "Breathe," the track they'd written together. Both women were fans of each other first, so having the opportunity to create something magical together for the album felt wonderful. Taylor told *That's Country* that "Breathe" was a "song about having to say goodbye to somebody, but it never blames anybody. Sometimes that's the most difficult part. When it's nobody's fault."

Suzie is twenty and from Trim in Ireland. Her favorite three songs are "Mean," "Shake It Off" and "Enchanted." Her favorite music video is 22 because it's just Taylor and her friends dancing and having fun!

She says: "It's not too bad, being a fan of Taylor in Ireland coz she's been here twice and we have an Irish Swiftie Squad and we're always meeting up and talking and stuff, so it's okay!"

Suzie met Taylor in Glasgow in June 2015. Tay had seen Suzie's Tumblr posts about making the trip from Ireland to Scotland just to see her and had asked her people to make contact with Suzie to see if they could meet up.

Suzie was so surprised when she got the call from Nashville and spent the rest of the day wandering around Glasgow in a daze. She explains: "I wasn't allowed to post about it online till after it happened though, which killed me, but when Taylor Swift's people ask you to do something, YOU DO IT.

"I was so excited when I collected my letter from the box office and joined two other girls who'd also been contacted by Taylor's people. Before long, a woman came up to us and said, 'Hey, are you Taylor's Tumblr friends?' Just hearing the word 'friends' made us feel really honored.

"She brought us to the front of the meet-and-greet line and I was the first to go in. The second Taylor saw me she shouted, 'SUZIE! Thanks for coming to so many shows!' I didn't even have to tell her my name, she knew!

"I started yapping about Dora and stuffed animal cats, and she didn't really understand me, but she was hugging me and stuff, and then we spoke about her Dublin concerts and she said, 'I'm so excited to go back for two shows.' And I told her about how much fun I was having on this trip and all the friends I've made on it, and the friends I've made in general coz of her. I got to say loads more but I kinda blanked out!

"I couldn't believe that one of the world's most powerful women wanted to meet me and cared so much to the point that she knew exactly who I was without me telling her. To all my Swiftie pals who think she's not seeing your posts and stuff . . . she is, and so is Taylor Nation, so keep posting. I'm the happiest person in the world right now because I got to meet Taylor."

Taylor has fans of all ages, and Remy from Gorey, County Wexford, is one of her youngest. She might only be three years old, but Remy's a huge Swiftie and loves dancing along to her favorite songs, "Shake It Off," "Blank Space" and "Style."

Remy and her mom Naomi filmed a really cute video message for Taylor when her 1989 Tour came to Dublin. To check it out for yourself, search for "Welcome Taylor Swift, biggest Irish fan sends kisses" on YouTube.

Naomi says: "Remy just loves everything about Taylor. She hasn't met many other fans yet because she's so young. I thought Remy was a little too young to go to the gig, so she wanted to send the video message, saying hi to Taylor.

"As far as I go, I do really like Taylor's music and I really admire how nice a person she is and that she takes time to meet her fans. She is the type of musician I want my little girl to look up to. We haven't been to a gig, but next time Taylor is in Dublin we are definitely going!"

CHAPTER 17
ITALY

Taylor's Italian fan base is very passionate and always tries to support her in whatever she's doing. On March 15, 2011, Taylor performed her Speak Now World Tour in Milan, but so far it's the only time she's toured in Italy. She didn't do any Italian dates on her Fearless, Red or 1989 Tours, which has been hugely disappointing for Italian fans. They had petitioned to get Taylor to visit them with 1989, but alas, it wasn't to be: Taylor's schedule was so packed, she couldn't make the trip.

If you're an Italian fan, make sure you become a fan of Taylor Swift Italia on Facebook and join the other 14,000 fans to find out the latest news about your favorite popstar.

DID YOU KNOW?

"Change" from Taylor's second album, *Fearless*, is about how hard she and her team had to work to get where they are today. Taylor admitted to Carla Hay from *The Examiner*: "There were times I was working so hard that I didn't realize that every single day our numbers were getting bigger. Every single day, our fan base was growing. Every single day, the work that we were doing was paying off. Then, during the 2007 CMA [Country Music Association] Awards, when they called out my name as the Horizon Award winner, I looked over and saw the president of my record label crying. Walking up those stairs, it just occurred to me that that was the night things changed. It changed everything."

Denise is twenty and from Reggio Emilia. Her favorite songs are "Shake It Off," "Love Story," "Fearless," "Sparks Fly" and "The Story Of Us." She admires Taylor for daring to dream big dreams and working so hard to become the successful singer she is today.

Denise says: "I first heard 'Love Story' when it was featured on the *Letters to Juliet* movie soundtrack. I really liked the song, but it was a couple years later that I became a real fan of Taylor's.

"In Italy, 'Shake It Off' and 'Blank Space' were certified platinum and gold, and 'We Are Never Ever Getting Back Together' went gold. Tay's Italian fan base is getting bigger and bigger all the time, which is so exciting. We'd love it if she visited more often but we understand that she's popular all around the world, so it's hard for her to find time to visit every country.

"I went all the way to Cologne, Germany, to see her 1989 show because I didn't want to miss out. I had to fly there and pay to stay in a hotel, but it was worth it. During the show, Taylor sang 'Style' right in front of me and gave me the biggest smile. It made me so happy. I think she liked the fox costumes me and my boyfriend were wearing—our photo is now on her official website, which feels amazing."

CHAPTER 18
MALAYSIA

Taylor brought her Red Tour to Malaysia in June 2014, when she performed for one night only at the Stadium Putra in Kuala Lumpur on June 11. It was right at the end of the tour, with only her Singapore performance to go, so her Malaysian fans had been patiently waiting months for their turn to see her play live.

Taylor might not have been back since, but Malaysian Swifties still enjoy watching videos of her latest performances and award shows online. They love it when Taylor shows how talented and funny she can be.

In 2009, she guest-hosted *Saturday Night Live*. Although they couldn't see the show on TV, Malaysian fans could join with fans from other countries to watch it. The show traditionally starts with an opening monologue by the person hosting.

This is normally provided for them because it's supposed to be really funny. Taylor could have taken the easy option and read from a script but she decided to write the monologue herself, in the form of a song. Her "Monologue Song" was very witty. It discussed lots of things she wasn't going to mention—such as Kanye West, glittery dresses, men who cheat on her, Joe Jonas, Taylor Lautner . . . it was wonderful! If you haven't seen it yet (or perhaps you haven't seen it in a while), you should definitely check it out on YouTube.

Ong is seventeen and is a boy Swiftie. He instantly became a fan when he first listened to "You Belong With Me" on the radio, back in 2009. His favorite music video is "Love Story" and his favorite three songs are "You Belong With Me," "If This Was A Movie" and "22."

Ong says: "I can't decide what I love about Taylor the most, I love everything! It is tough, being a Swiftie in Malaysia because Taylor doesn't come here very often and all the merchandise has to be imported in, so that means it's much more expensive than in other countries, but Malaysian Swifties are just as passionate about Taylor as fans in other countries.

"I had the privilege of going to see Taylor in Kuala Lumpur as part of her Red Tour and I'll never forget it. It was awesome! Words cannot describe how I felt as I stood in the stadium, waiting for the show to start—I was overcome with emotion.

"We all united, every single fan joined in, singing along and dancing, all night long. Club Red was set up, but due to her tight schedule, she had to leave early to get to Singapore for the final show of the tour, so it was canceled. I was disappointed, but considering some Swifties don't even have the chance to watch her live, I'm still grateful."

Aiera is fifteen and from Kuala Lumpur. Her favorite three songs are "You're Not Sorry," "Blank Space" and "Haunted." She says: "I love it when Taylor smiles. She's so beautiful and so talented, her songs are incredible. Listening to them makes me so happy.

"I actually became a fan after an ex-boyfriend of mine recommended her music to me. He suggested I listened to 'Red' and 'Begin Again.' I was hooked from then on. Her lyrics in these songs are really deep. She's a really talented songwriter and isn't afraid to write about real-life experiences.

"Malaysian Swifties are super amazing and awesome. We make sure we keep up to date with the latest Tay news and we're just like a big family. Getting hold of posters, books, T-shirts and other merchandise is difficult in our country, but we're just as devoted as fans in other countries. We will support Tay, no matter what."

CHAPTER 19

THE NETHERLANDS

Taylor brought her Speak Now World Tour to the Netherlands on March 7, 2011. She performed at the Ahoy in Rotterdam to almost 5,000 of her biggest Dutch fans. The only European dates for her Red Tour were in England and Germany, but for her *1989* show she came back, performing at the Ziggo Dome in Amsterdam on June 21, 2015.

When a journalist from the *Metro Niews* was due to do a phone interview with Taylor a few days before her Amsterdam show, her assistant had to ring him and ask for his phone number again. The day before, she'd written his number on a napkin and Taylor had used it to wipe her forehead and no longer had it! He didn't mind giving his number again—if anything, he felt honored that his number had touched Taylor's forehead!

When Taylor rang him that evening at home she started the call by saying: "Hey, this is Taylor. Are you Mario?"

One of the questions he asked was, "Where is the craziest place you've ever heard one of your songs?" She replied: "Several times, when I've been on a vacation on a remote tropical island and sipping a drink in an equally secluded beach shack, I've suddenly heard a song by myself on the radio. It's very nice, especially when you least expect it. And it's always great to hear that you are being played on the radio. It's a reward for hard work."

He then asked what Dutch fans could expect from her 1989 show, and she said in response: "It is a very visual show with lights, choreography and costumes based on the songs of *1989*, supplemented by a few older songs."

DID YOU KNOW?

Taylor had always wanted to act in an episode of crime show *CSI* and she got her wish in 2009! The show's producer, Carol Mendelsohn, contacted her after she had heard that Taylor was a fan, and asked Taylor to play an edgy character called Haley Jones, which she loved. She shared on her MySpace page: "When I'm really old and can only remember one story about my life to go back and relive and tell over and over and over again to the point where my grandchildren roll their eyes and leave the room—that's the story."

Demi is twenty and from Amsterdam. She's been a Swiftie for seven years and her favorite songs are "Shake It off," "The Last Time" and "Blank Space." Demi loves being a Dutch Swiftie and was one of the first, as Taylor has only become hugely popular there in the last year. Her concert for the 1989 Tour on June 21 in Amsterdam was a sell-out, but Demi managed to get tickets with her family. Demi says: "Just before I became a Swiftie I was diagnosed with Friedreich's ataxia, which is a rare disease that affects the nervous system, and a serious heart condition that means I have had to spend lots of time in hospital.

"I was lucky enough to meet Taylor four years ago, on June 11, 2011, thanks to the Make-A-Wish Foundation. They flew me, my parents and my sister Sam over to America, because meeting Taylor was my one big dream. When we arrived in Detroit, we were picked up by limousine, which was amazing. It made me feel like a star! We were driven to a shop to meet Taylor, but the meet-and-greet line was so long. Thankfully, I was allowed to go first and Taylor spent time chatting to me, signing her autograph and posing for photos.

"Afterward, I was taken into a room and shown some of Taylor's dresses and shoes—they were beautiful. An assistant came to speak to me and then we went into the T-party room. As we went inside, Taylor came around the corner and said, 'Hi, Demi.' I was so happy, I found it hard to speak. She gave me a hug and I managed to hand her a book I had made with other Dutch Swifties. She loved it, telling me she thought it was beautiful and she couldn't wait to read it.

"She was so kind and lovely. She happily posed for photos with my family. It was such a special day for us all—I'll never forget it. She told me she loved me and I was overcome with emotion, I was so happy. I loved having the opportunity to see her perform live in concert just an hour later—she really is one in a million and I'll be a Swiftie forever."

Eline is twenty-four and from Bergeijk. Her favorite three songs are "Long Live," "Fearless" and "Today Was A Fairytale." She says: "My favorite music video would be *We Are Never Ever Getting Back Together*. I love it because it's such a fun and cheery video and the whole band is in it. The fact that they filmed it in one take is just amazing and I love Taylor's attitude in it.

"It's hard to remember how I became a fan; it was such a long time ago. In the beginning of 2009, I was obsessed with American pop culture and at that time listened to Demi Lovato and Selena Gomez a lot. I don't even know how I came across Tay's music but I was immediately hooked for life. I was a hopeless romantic when I was seventeen and heartbroken about a boyfriend breaking up with me, so I loved listening to Taylor's music.

"What she's managed to achieve in her career so far has been amazing—I can't wait to see what she'll achieve in the next five, ten years. I do hope to meet her one day, but I know the chances are slim because I'm not very active on Twitter or Tumblr. I may be slightly older than the average Swiftie but I don't care what other people outside of the fandom think. I just want to fangirl over Tay."

Marinka is twenty-five and from Zwaag. A Swiftie for seven years, she was one of Tay's first fans in the Netherlands. She discovered Tay's music after she heard "White Horse" being played on her favorite TV show, *Grey's Anatomy*, and it will always be a special song to her because of this.

Marinka joined together with a handful of other Dutch Swifties and in 2010 they held their first fan event. There were only six people at the first event, but since then she and her friends have organized many other fan events and they usually have between fifty and sixty fans in attendance.

Marinka says: "I really love 'Tim McGraw,' 'Enchanted' and 'The Moment I Knew,' but there are just too many great songs to choose from. My favorite songs kind of change from day-to-day. One of my favorite songs from *Speak Now* is 'If This Was A Movie,' which is sadly the only song on the entire record she's never played live.

"As of today I've been to twelve of Taylor's shows and have met her twice (the second time is by far the best day of my life so far). This is my story:

MARCH 7, 2011—SPEAK NOW WORLD TOUR—ROTTERDAM, THE NETHERLANDS—T-PARTY

"The first time I saw Taylor live was when she came to the Netherlands with her Speak Now World Tour. The place wasn't sold out. In fact, the second level of the venue was closed with curtains so it seemed kind of full, but people who know there's a second level knew better. I was one of the first people to arrive.

"I'd arrived at half past seven and met up with some Swifties I'd been chatting to online because none of my other friends were fans. We had a blast, singing her songs and talking about her. When she arrived at the venue we sang her songs and took pictures with her band members and her mom. Taylor walked by quickly and didn't take photos with anyone, but at least we got a glimpse of her.

"The concert was standing room on the floor, so we were the lucky ones to get front-row because we were at the venue so early. I was standing center stage right in front of the catwalk. The moment she came onstage I freaked out and cried because I just couldn't believe she was right there in front of me. I had been a fan for nearly three years and it was the first time I'd seen her in real life performing. It was amazing! During the song 'Back To December', a woman came up to my friend and asked if we wanted to meet Taylor. We started crying and jumping and screaming. We couldn't believe we were going to meet her, and the rest of the show was just a blur because meeting Taylor was all we could think about.

"After the show we were welcomed into the 'T-party.' There was pizza, a Ping-Pong table and a TV that played Taylor's videos. The room looked so beautiful. We hadn't had anything to eat or to drink for seven hours, so we helped ourselves to the pizza and treats. We talked to Paul Sidoti, Amos Heller and Grant Mickelson before Taylor walked into the room. Paul, Amos and Grant are Tay's guitarists and bass player and they were so friendly.

"Taylor was dressed casually, with hardly any makeup on and a ponytail. Everyone got a few minutes with her and the opportunity to have a photo taken. When I walked up to her, her first words were 'Wow! You're so tall! I love it!' (Yes, I'm taller than Taylor; I'm 6' 1" and Taylor is 5' 10".) Besides saying thank you and I love you a few times, I couldn't really speak properly because I was so overwhelmed by the situation. Tay was so lovely, she was smiling and giving us compliments and signing her autograph. Before we knew it, it was over: the whole night was just a blur."

GET TAYLOR ON AIR

"On my way home I couldn't help but feel sorry for my best friend Sylvia, who was a huge Swiftie but hadn't been able to come to the concert because she was competing in the final of a talent show that very night. I felt so bad, but thankfully her time would come and she would meet Taylor in 2013. (I'll tell you what happened later!)

"After the concert I decided with some fellow Swifties that we should create a Taylor Swift fan club. We had two main goals: to arrange fan events so we could meet up again and meet new Swifties and to encourage radio stations to play Taylor's music.

"We began by tweeting radio stations, requesting her songs at set times so those radio stations would receive hundreds of tweets about Taylor in a few minutes and we couldn't go unnoticed. We had limited success but we didn't give up.

"We organized fan events at random parks so we could just hang out. We talked about Taylor, brought along guitars and we sang her songs and sometimes we even remade some of her best videos. To see the videos for yourself, check out our YouTube channel GetTaylorOnAir."

MARCH 12, 2011—SPEAK NOW WORLD TOUR—OBERHAUSEN, GERMANY

"So actually, we bought these tickets before buying tickets for Rotterdam. The tour date for Oberhausen was announced earlier and by that time we didn't know if she was coming to the Netherlands at all, so we bought tickets to see her in Germany. Turned out, this meant we could see her twice! This time my best friend Sylvia DID come and we had a blast. We ran over to the B-stage during Taylor's set there, and when Taylor walked past me, she looked into my eyes and said, 'You came again, I love you!' She looked at me and Sylvia during an entire verse of 'Fifteen' and because of that moment 'Fifteen' will always be a special song to us."

JULY 23, 2011—SPEAK NOW WORLD TOUR—NEWARK, NEW JERSEY, USA

"I was going to visit a friend in Toronto, Canada, and we decided to book a weekend to New York while Taylor was performing there. I found out that the Speak Now Tour was very different in the USA and it DID include three of my favorite songs from *Speak Now* that weren't included in the European concerts ('Mean,' 'Last Kiss' and 'Haunted'). My friend went with me because I wanted to go. She liked it, but she's not a Swiftie. I had fun, but you just don't let go the way you do when you are with a real Swiftie, so my advice to any Swiftie would be: if you go to a concert, go with a Swiftie! Even if you don't know him/her very well, you'll probably have more fun than if you went with someone you DO know but who is not that into her."

RED

"In 2012, Taylor's fourth studio album [*Red*] came out and something I thought was impossible happened: Taylor put out a song that I didn't actually like. I was confused and didn't know if I could still call myself a Swiftie when there was clearly something I didn't like. It got worse because 'We Are Never

Ever Getting Back Together' was somehow the first song that got a lot of airplay in the Netherlands. All those people who knew I was a fan of Taylor but had never heard one song of hers now thought I was a big fan of THIS kind of music. Let me tell you, I'm NOT! Over time I've gotten to appreciate the song a little bit more, but to date 'We Are Never Ever Getting Back Together' is still by FAR my least favorite song of hers, like ever!

"Luckily, I liked the rest of the album, especially her collaboration with Ed Sheeran, another artist I hugely admire."

JULY19, 2013—RED WORLD TOUR—PHILADELPHIA, PENNSYLVANIA, USA

"When Taylor announced her tour dates for the Red Tour and that Ed Sheeran was going to be supporting her in America, I was so excited. I knew I had to plan to see the show there, so together with my parents, I got planning. Sadly, my mom got a hernia, which meant that she couldn't go to the show, and my dad had to look after her, but I still went on my own. At a Taylor Swift concert you're never 'by yourself.' There were so many great Swifties there and I made a bunch of friends that day. The show was amazing!"

JULY 26, 2013—RED WORLD TOUR—FOXBOROUGH, MASSACHUSETS, USA—CLUB RED

"A week after the Philadelphia show, I met up with Sylvia in Boston and we drove to our hotel near Foxborough. We wanted something to stand out in the stadium, so we stopped by a store to buy supplies for a sign. We practically spent about the entire day in our hotel room working on a sign that said: 'We-e went 3470 miles to get back together' (based on the song lyrics of 'We Are Never Ever Getting Back Together'). I was so happy to be with my best friend and to be able to share this amazing experience with her. When we got to Gillette, our minds were blown: this was THE stadium we knew from her documentary, *Journey to Fearless*, and from the epic 'rainshow' that features in her *Sparks Fly* music video!

"So many people had come dressed up and had signs. It was amazing to see what everyone had come up with. I had so much fun! We figured there was no chance at all of us getting Club Red since there were like 55,000 other people wanting the same thing, but somehow, by some magical twist of fate during 'I Knew You Were Trouble,' Andrea Swift walked by. We thought she was passing us, but she turned her head to read our signs and then she came over to Sylvia. I think my heart stopped for a moment when Andrea asked Sylvia if she had ever met Taylor before. Well, of course she hadn't! She hadn't gone to that show in the Netherlands. And so, we were given bracelets and invited to Club Red. I couldn't believe it. We cried and cried and screamed and just hugged each other while jumping up and down.

"Once we were in Club Red, we saw Paul Sidoti and started talking to him. We talked about how the band got together, about Holland and about a Dutch band called Van Halen (someone he knows is in the band). He said he likes all of Taylor's music, but he's in love with Taylor's first album [*Taylor Swift*] the most. We chatted about whether he gets recognized a lot when he's out in public, about GetTaylorOnAir and about how he'll stay in Taylor's band as long as Taylor wants him in it. He also told us how the acoustic version of 'Teardrops On My Guitar' was created in a hotel room, for the MTV acoustic performance with him, Taylor and Grant. We took a picture with him, he said goodbye to us and he left Club Red.

"Next to us, Taylor's dad, Scott Swift, was talking to someone. We waited patiently and started a conversation with him. He asked us how we got in and we showed him our signs. He was blown away by the fact we came all the way from Holland, so he gave us all the guitar picks he had left in his pocket. 'I'm sorry, these are all I have left,' he said. He was so nice and gave us another spectacular gift—pit tickets for the next day! We were lucky enough to get third-level seats (because it sold out so fast we didn't even have tickets at all at first), but Scott had given us passes to go stand in the PIT! Like front row in front of the stage! We absolutely fell in love with Scott Swift—he is so awesome and he's just like Taylor describes him. He's so enthusiastic and proud of her, it was amazing to see. She has the nicest dad.

"We were having such a lovely time in Club Red and then Ed Sheeran walked in, making it even better than we thought possible. We managed to have a short conversation with him, we told him how talented he is and that we'd already seen him live in Holland. 'Oh, so you were at the Heineken Music Hall?' he asked.

'Yes!' we replied, 'but we also went to that very first show in De Melkweg.'

'You went to that one?! Oh, my gosh, you are real fans! I've got fans! That's awesome!' Then he high-fived us, took a picture, gave us a hug and he left Club Red.

"We started talking to other Swifties about how crazy it was to be there. By that time Taylor had arrived in Club Red, but we were told that she would make her way around the room and she would come up to you and not the other way around. So we were just waiting patiently, talking to the other Swifties.

"We were almost the last ones to talk to Taylor. There was one more group after us. Taylor walked up, gave us a hug and said to me: 'Wow! You're really tall!' (Wait, I've heard that before, lol!) We talked about Holland and Taylor told us to tell everybody back in Holland thanks for everything, 'cause she thought everybody there had been so wonderful. We talked about our favorite songs. We asked if there would ever be a Fearless Tour DVD, 'cause *Journey to Fearless* doesn't have all the songs in it. She said she would think about it. We asked her why she didn't do 'Stay Stay Stay.' This was kind of a big deal since the song was included in the setlist but somehow she didn't play it the second night in Philly and neither did she in Foxborough, so the entire fandom was kind of speculating what had happened. She answered that they started missing curfews on the building. And it was a technical thing they had to pay overtime. So they had to cut one song and if she had to cut one, 'Stay Stay Stay' would be it. Sylvia told her she became a singer-songwriter because of her. Taylor wished her good luck and said she hoped she would have her song on her iPod one day. Well, that would be awesome!

"And that was it—the best five minutes of our lives! She was so amazing and nice. And we got to say basically everything we wanted to say. No regrets. To see a video we made of our experience, search for the Sylvia Aimee channel on YouTube."

JULY 27, 2013—RED WORLD TOUR—FOXBOROUGH, MASSACHUSETTS, USA

"So yeah, the next day we were standing so close to the stage that we could actually touch it. Taylor looked us right in the eye twice and Paul recognized us too. Taylor played 'Fearless' on the B-stage, which is a special song for Sylvia and me because we both became Swifties in the *Fearless* era and that's also when we met each other. It was amazing! I can't say any more about it."

FEBRUARY 1, 2014—RED WORLD TOUR—LONDON, UK

"In 2014, Taylor actually did come to Europe with the Red Tour so we just had to go again. GetTaylorOnAir was now a pretty large fan group and over 40 Dutch Swifties from our group were flying to London to see Taylor! The members of our fan club are so dedicated."It was a great night and the best surprise was that Ed Sheeran was the special guest and he performed 'Lego House' with Taylor."

FEBRUARY 2, 2014—RED WORLD TOUR—LONDON, UK

"When you fly to London to go to a concert, you might as well go twice!"

JUNE 19, 2015—1989 WORLD TOUR—COLOGNE, GERMANY

"*1989* came out and even though I'm usually more into Tay's country songs than pop songs, I fell completely in love with this new record. As soon as she announced the tour dates, me and my friends immediately started planning our trips. We would see the show for the first time in Germany, in an arena four hours from where I live."

JUNE 21, 2015—1989 WORLD TOUR—AMSTERDAM, THE NETHERLANDS

"She came to the Netherlands again! This time around, it was sold out. We arrived at the venue pretty early because we'd organized a Swiftie meeting there. Lots of Swifties from GetTaylorOnAir joined us and we all played guitars, sang and took part in a Taylor Swift Quiz, with Taylor merchandise for the winners.

"One of the members of GetTaylorOnAir actually won a meet and greet with Taylor before the show. We made Taylor a cookbook with recipes from all the Swifties in our fan club, and the girl who got to meet Taylor gave it to her.

"When we went to stand in line to get into the venue we spotted Amos Heller [Taylor's bass guitar player], standing in a café. We walked up to him and chatted with him for, like, half an hour. He was so awesome—he told us he's way more into *1989* than any of Taylor's previous albums and that he loves the 1989 Tour. We talked about all kinds of other stuff, like music, being in a studio and recording. It's really awesome that he took so much time to talk to us. We were kind of wondering why there weren't that many other Swifties coming up to him, but I guess only the Swifties that have been there since the era in which Taylor made all those video blogs and stuff really know her band members. Anyway, the night was flawless (obviously) and when I walked out, I was so glad this wasn't my last time seeing the 1989 Tour."

JULY 24, 2015—1989 WORLD TOUR—FOXBOROUGH, MASSACHUSETTS, USA

"So yeah, since my super-awesome experience in 2013 took place at Gillette, I just had to come back. One of my other Swiftie friends wanted to join me, so we took a two-week trip to the US and made sure the concert was at the end of our trip ('cause that would be the highlight). Taylor sold out Gillette for two nights in a row again, so obviously we went both times. It was incredible and just so much better than the show in the Netherlands because this venue is about three times as big and with all the glowing bracelets, it's just a thousand times more beautiful with more people."

JULY 25, 2015—1989 WORLD TOUR—FOXBOROUGH, MASSACHUSETTS, USA

"I still hope that Taylor decides to do another European leg of this tour so I can see it again, but for now I guess this was my last time seeing the show. I had a great time!"

"I'd like to finish my story by describing what it's like to be a Dutch Swiftie. Being a Swiftie in the Netherlands is very different to being one in the UK or the US, I think. First of all, except for 'Love Story,' they never played ANY song of Taylor's on the radio until *Red* came out. Before 2010, practically no one had ever heard about her (except some kids who knew her because she's friends with Selena Gomez and Demi Lovato, I guess). Anyway, when she did get played on the radio, it was when she was dating Harry Styles that she got most of the attention.

"I was kind of bummed that they never talked about all the things she'd accomplished on the radio. They just talked about her dating life, which made everyone who doesn't really know her believe she was some kind of a serial dater, which she's not. I think it's kind of sad that a lot of people I know just know about her boyfriends and not about her music. 'We Are Never Getting Back Together' and 'Trouble' were played on the radio, but songs like 'Begin Again' and 'Red' never made it here since they were labeled 'country.' I kind of hate our radio stations for just playing pop songs. Songs like 'Red' and 'Sparks Fly' would fit really well on the radio here, in my opinion, so I just don't get why they don't play them.

"A lot has changed since *1989* came out, because that album is all pop, so they have been playing her songs ever since 'Shake It Off' came out. Now everybody knows who she is. But I'm still bummed most people don't know her beautiful country songs and just know the easy-to-sing-along-to pop songs on the new record. But, hey, at least they know who she is now. I still hope she goes back to making country music someday and that radio stations in Europe will play those songs, because I know there are a lot of people here who love that kind of music too.

"So as of today I'm still a huge fan of Taylor. I'm glad our fan club has grown and is still alive after all these years. I've made so many friends because of GetTaylorOnAir and we do lots of fun stuff together. A lot of Swifties in that group went to see Taylor in different countries and a lot of them even traveled to the USA to see her. I really hope Taylor comes back here soon to give us another amazing show!"

Demi is fifteen and from Rotterdam. Her favorite three songs are "I Wish You Would," "Come Back Be Here" and "Sparks Fly." She says: "I [officially] became a fan in 2012. I already knew who she was in 2007 because of her debut hit, 'Love Story,' but I hadn't discovered the 'fandom thing' yet. I was twelve when I became a fan of hers and it was mainly because of Twitter. I started getting into the fandom thing and I started listening to her music (because loads of people tweeted about how good it was!) and I was hooked.

"What I love about Taylor the most is her loyalty to her fans and how she is always so kind to people. She treats everyone (from fans to friends to family) equally and she seems to be a nice person to hang out with and be friends with. She is so bubbly, so honest, and I love her sparkling personality. She is also really charming and she has this kind of charisma that makes people fall in love with her. She's such a beautiful person, inside and out, and it's cheesy, but there's no other way to say it.

"For me, the best thing about being a Dutch Swiftie is all the Dutch fans I've met. They've become some of my closest friends. We love Taylor so much and we're really devoted to her. We love it when she visits our country because everyone gets so excited."

CHAPTER 20

NEW ZEALAND

Taylor brought her Speak Now and Red Tours to New Zealand, performing at the Vector Arena in Auckland. She actually closed her Speak Now Tour in the country and has always loved meeting her Kiwi fans. Despite this, she didn't bring her 1989 Tour to New Zealand, which was a real shame. Her Kiwi Swifties were disappointed but many traveled to nearby Australia to see a show instead.

DID YOU KNOW?

Taylor is really good friends with Kiwi singer-songwriter Lorde. They sang Lorde's hit "Royals" together at her 1989 show in Washington. Taylor was so thankful that Lorde had flown for nineteen hours just to be there, and tweeted afterward that she was a "wondrous angel."

In November 2015, many people expected to see Taylor at the American Music Awards but she didn't go and instead jetted off on a well-deserved break to New Zealand. She didn't announce where she was going and news only broke when a couple of people spotted her at Auckland airport.

If you're a Swiftie who lives in New Zealand, make sure you join the NZ Taylor Swift Fans page on Facebook to find out about the latest Taylor news and special events.

> DID YOU KNOW?
>
> In the video for "Shake It Off" Taylor dresses up as Lady Gaga, Fergie, Gwen Stefani and Skrillex.

Mia is eleven years old and from Hamilton. Her favorite three songs are "Love Story," "Blank Space" and "22." She says: "'Love Story' has to be in my top three because this is the one that started it all for me. I remember when I was four and a half years old and I saw a little bit of the music video on television and I thought she looked so pretty in her princess dress (I was into Disney princesses at the time), so this was amazing for me to see what I thought was a real-life princess. Ever since then I have been a Swiftie. I call myself New Zealand's Number 1 Swiftie!

"'Blank Space' is another of my favorites, as it is such an awesome song with catchy lyrics, amazing vocals and a good beat. '22' makes me want to get up and dance whenever I hear it—I like that it is all about having fun and hanging out with friends, which describes my life a lot at present.

"My favorite music video is *Bad Blood* because it is so cool, such a different look for Taylor. I love the whole background behind it and the way she can also display her acting skills at the same time. I really like the fact that she asked [hip hop recording artist] Kendrick Lamar to feature in the video and to sing, to change up the song a bit, so different for her, but in a good way—it really worked so well. It's also cool that she had so many of her real-life friends in the video. It's a masterpiece!

"What I love about Taylor Swift the most is that she writes songs that are so relatable to so many people all around the world. Also, she is such a nice person, so kind, caring, genuine, generous, giving, who seems to put others before herself. She loves her family, she's happy to meet fans, goes to hospitals to cheer up sick children, donates to people in need. Also, she is a fantastic role model for a girl my age, someone I can look up to and admire; she understands that too and takes on the role responsibly. She makes the world a better place and the world is lucky to have the music of Taylor Swift. I also like her fashion!

"What I like about being a Swiftie here in New Zealand is the fact that her physical album is released here first as timewise we are ahead here in the eastern hemisphere. My mom always takes me to the shop early before it's even open to get my copy—it's not even on the shelves yet. We have been the first people to buy her last two albums, *1989* and *Red*, here in Hamilton.

"I've not met Taylor yet, but I've been to both her concerts here in New Zealand, which were absolutely amazing. My first concert ever at age seven was Speak Now in 2012 (it was also my mum's first ever concert too), then Red in 2013—a couple of very cool things did happen for me!!!!

"At her Speak Now Tour on March 17, 2012 in Auckland she was on the balcony hovering over the crowd, performing 'Love Story,' and I was waving so much with both arms waving crazily, then she waved back and I couldn't believe it, I was so happy. I didn't stop going on about it for ages, made my night.

"Then at her Red Tour on November 30, 2013, before the show started I saw Mama Swift [Taylor's mum, Andrea] walking through the crowds. We had such great seats I was able to quickly run down the aisle and I touched her hand. I felt so lucky. Then while Taylor was performing '22,' she was being carried around the arena by some bodyguards. I ran so fast back down the stairs of the aisle I thought my legs would fall off, but it paid off as I made eye contact with her and I smiled! My arms were a bit short to reach her hand and I was pushed around a bit by other fans, but it was worth it. That was an awesome moment for me—I didn't stop going on about that for ages either!

"I hope to one day meet Taylor. It would be my dream come true! I'm really dedicated and traveled with my mum to see her 1989 show in Melbourne, Australia, because she wasn't performing any New Zealand dates. It was an incredible show and I'm really glad I didn't miss out. I really hope she comes back to New Zealand for her next tour, though—we need her!"

Ella is fifteen and from Tauranga, New Zealand. Her favorite three songs are "Clean," "A Place In This World" and "Shake It Off." She says: " 'Clean' is my favorite because it is such a relaxing song and I can really relate to it with my own journey. I love the song 'A Place In This World' from her first album as it describes how I feel, growing up in such a tough, judgemental world and trying to figure out how I fit in and what I want to do. And my third favorite is, of course, 'Shake It Off.' It inspires me to ignore the haters and bullies, and live my life and not worry about what they think.

"My favorite music video is *The Best Day*. I like this music video so much because it's not the kind of music video you see often. It shows home videos of Taylor as a kid and her mom, which I think is adorable!

"Being a Swiftie in New Zealand is pretty cool, but at the same time we miss out on a lot of stuff because we are such a small country. We don't get as much merchandise as other countries so when we find some, it's like finding gold! Being a Swiftie when she comes to New Zealand, though, is one of the most amazing things as our arena is quite small, so even if you're at the very back of the arena, which I was at her Red Tour, you're still quite close to her and she seems to really love New Zealand!

"Sadly, we missed out on the 1989 Tour for whatever reason, which is heartbreaking because we all wanted her to come so badly. I see a lot of Swiftie meet-ups that happen in places like London and New York and we have tried holding them in Auckland, but since everyone is so spread out and there's not many of us, it's so hard to hold a meet-up. Hopefully, we'll be able to do one someday soon.

"I will never forget going to see Taylor perform her Speak Now Tour in 2012 with my mum and friend Alyssa. We had seats on the side, very close to the stage and the end of the row and above her dressing room! We were some of the first people seated and at one point we heard a voice that sounded like Taylor's mum. So we looked over the side and we saw Taylor and her mum walking into her room, so we called out her name and she looked up and smiled and waved at us. I've also had two of my posts on Instagram liked by Taylor in the past! It was such a surprise when she liked them. I had to keep clicking on her "like" and checking it was really her, then I had dozens of comments from Swifties around the world that had seen that Taylor had liked my photos and wanted to congratulate me. I cannot thank Taylor enough for these moments and they are moments I will treasure forever!"

Taylor is twenty and from Matamata. Her favorite three songs are "All Too Well," "Sad Beautiful Tragic" and "Clean." She says: "My favorite three music videos are *I Knew You Were Trouble*, because it has an amazing intro, *Fifteen* as it was the first video clip I ever saw of Taylor, and *Shake It Off*, because she's being herself throughout the whole video.

"The thing I love about Taylor the most is her attitude towards her fans—she loves us all as much as we love her. Her music pretty much saved my life. It's amazing to be a fan in New Zealand. So many people support Taytay over here, and we were all really upset when she didn't bring her 1989 Tour here.

"I've been lucky enough to see her perform live twice. I attended her Speak Now Tour with a friend when I was sixteen, and the Red Tour with my best friend when I was seventeen. They were the most amazing nights of my life!

"Both of the concerts I went to were at The Vector Arena in Auckland, New Zealand. I remember walking into the venue for the Speak Now Tour (this was my first Taylor concert) and the whole place smelled like Wonderstruck (her perfume, which had just been released). Girls were walking around, handing out little samples of the perfume and smellies to hang from your car mirrors! I've still got all of the stuff I collected from her concerts. When the show started, I shed a few tears because I couldn't believe that I was actually seeing my idol in the flesh! My favorite part of the Speak Now Tour was when she performed 'Haunted.' She had a beautiful, ripped-up blood-red dress on and she sounded absolutely amazing! The performers around her were hanging from these giant bells, and that amazed me. Also, that night Taylor performed her song 'Eyes Open' for the first time in concert. I thought that was pretty special too!

"My favorite moment from the Red Tour would have to be when she performed 'All Too Well'—the way she played the piano and flicked her hair, it was breathtaking! I got an awesome photo of Taylor standing about sixty feet away from me at one point. I'll treasure it forever."

CHAPTER 21

THE PHILIPPINES

Taylor performed her Speak Now World Tour at the Smart Araneta Coliseum, Manila on February 19, 2011 in front of an audience of over 12,000. She came back in 2014 with her Red Tour, performing at the Mall of Asia Arena on June 6 to a slightly smaller audience of 10,000 fans. Sadly, she didn't manage to visit with her 1989 World Tour.

Filipino fans have a fantastic website (www. taylor-swiftph.com), as well as a great Facebook page. Their website was set up by superfan Odette Lia Agustin on August 20, 2008 and explains where fans can go to buy the latest Tay merchandise and what fan events are planned.

The website and Facebook page are managed by fourteen dedicated Swifties. They've helped to organize and promote several fan parties, get-togethers and album promotions in the last seven years, and in 2011 they met Taylor, her parents and her crew at her Manila show.

Together with other Asian Taylor Swift fan clubs they created the #REDTourAsiaMovement fan video in June 2014. It was coordinated by @TaylorSwiftSingapore and involved fans from six countries. You should check it out on YouTube; it's brilliant! To see so many fans joining together to sing "We Are Never Ever Getting Back Together" and showing their love in this way is really exciting.

Before the Red show, they encouraged Filipino fans to get involved in the *Para Kay Taylor* fan project (Give for Taylor Fan Project). More than seven hundred people took part, sending in a special Instagram photo of themselves, which the organizers painstakingly printed off and cut into wallet-sized photos. At the concert they presented the photos to a member of Tay's management team to give to her and during the performance they received the following message from Taylor herself before she sang "Mean": "Manila . . . We really love you. You are so giving, and so kind, and so creative . . . I have a lot of Instagram friends from the Philippines . . . and I have a lot of people who have sent me or given me presents from Manila, from the Philippines . . . And I wanted to say thank you for that."

Jennel is seventeen and is a huge Swiftie. Her favorite three songs are "Mine," "The Moment I Knew" and "Dear John." She says: "Being a fan in the Philippines is very difficult because Taylor is thousands of miles away, but there are lots of fans here and we're a community. We are proud to be Taylor's fans because she is so kind, sweet and super talented.

"We love listening to her albums and watching her music videos online. My favorite video is *Mine* because we get a glimpse of what it'll be like when Taylor is a mom. Taylor loves her own mom so much that it'll be exciting to see what she's like when she's a mom someday.

DID YOU KNOW?

"Mine" was a song that Taylor wrote about her tendency to run from love. Taylor and her studio team loved working on the track and as soon as she played it for Scott for the first time in his office, he was hooked. He told *Billboard*: "I'm jumping around playing air guitar, she's singing the song back to me, and it was just one of those crazy, fun, Taylor teenage moments." After the song came out, Taylor got an email from the guy it was about and he wrote, "I had no idea. I realize I've been naive."

"Tay is a talented actress and she shows this in her videos. I think the character she plays in the *Blank Space* video is quite a complex character but Tay pulls her off brilliantly. When she's damaging the car and slashing the portrait, you really feel the anger and betrayal she feels.

"Another favorite video of mine is *The Story Of Us*. I think most teenage girls can relate to what's happening in this video, and Tay looks super cute!"Vhida is fourteen and has been a Swiftie for the past five years. Her favorite songs are "Clean," "Shake It Off" and "Fearless." She says: "I love 'Clean' because through it Taylor teaches us that whatever happens we should stay strong and believe that we can achieve what we want to achieve. I love 'Shake It Off' because, like her, I just wanna take a break and enjoy life. 'Fearless' is special to me because it's about love and I know that one day I'll meet my Prince Charming.

"Taylor is a brilliant songwriter and I feel I can relate to everything she talks about in her songs. Like Taylor, I also loved someone who could not stay. What I love about Taylor the most is her attitude towards life. She never gives up in life even though she has many storms and trials that block her way. She is really fearless and her music has had a big impact on my life. By listening to her songs, I've learned many valuable life lessons.

"I admire her because even though she's famous, she is still down to earth. She tries her best to give her fans what they want, she follows as many as she can on Twitter and offers advice freely. She goes on tour all around the world to try to meet as many Swifties as she can. I really hope I can meet her one day so I can thank her for all she does for fans everywhere.

"Being a fan in the Philippines is really cool but it does test your patience and determination at times. You want Taylor to notice your country and visit, but so many fans message her every day that it's hard for you to stand out. I've been a Swiftie for five years but I never lose hope that I'll be noticed by Taylor one day."

CHAPTER 22

POLAND

Taylor has never visited Poland but she has lots of fans in the country. If you're a Polish Swiftie, make sure you become a fan of Taylor Swift Poland on Facebook. There are currently more than 5,000 fans of the page and you can join in with a fun scrapbook project for Taylor.

> DID YOU KNOW?
>
> Lots of Taylor's friends appear in her *Bad Blood* video and she let each one choose their character's name. The names chosen included Arsyn (Selena Gomez), Destructa X (Ellie Goulding), Frostbyte (Lily Aldridge), Knockout (Karlie Kloss), Headmistress (Cindy Crawford), Lucky Fiori (Lena Dunham) and Domino (Jessica Alba).

Zuzanna is seventeen and from Warsaw. She says: "It's so hard to try and pick my favorite three songs because I think Taylor is one of the best artists to ever exist. I would say 'Love Story' is one of my favorites because that was the first song of hers that I heard and it always reminds me of the moment I fell in love with her. I also adore 'Enchanted' because of its uniqueness and magical kind of mysterious beat, which leaves us wanting to know how the story of the song ends. My third choice is 'The Lucky One.' It helps me a lot and I can relate to it; it's also amazingly written.

"My favorite music video is probably *Shake It Off*. I remember when she posted it and everybody freaked out. It was the beginning of a new era and she seemed happier than ever.

"There are loads of things that I love about Taylor. I love how she's a normal girl who loves cats, music and meeting her fans. Of course she's made some mistakes, but she always wants to fix herself. I've looked up to her since I was about eleven, and that was one of the best decisions I ever made, because her music, her words, and just who she is as a person, always make me feel better.

"Being a Swiftie in Poland is probably a bit different from being an American or an English fan. But it's all right. There are actually lots of fans of Taylor here and I've made some good friends. She hasn't been to our country yet, but we still love her and wait for her to come one day."

Dominik is eighteen and from Grudziadz. His favorite three songs are "The Moment I Knew," "Wonderland" and "Eyes Open." He says: "I love these songs because I can identify with them. It's like Taylor is me, she's gone through the same things that I've gone through. Her videos are incredible too. I particularly like the videos for *White Horse*, *Blank Space* and *Everything Has Changed*. Every video she does is so creative and suits the song that she's singing.

"Tay's a wonderful person and artist. She visits sick fans in hospitals all around the world and she sends Swifties surprise gifts. She treats us as friends, not fans. She's one in a million. She isn't afraid to be different to other pop stars and teaches us all to embrace who we are.

"I hope she comes to Poland one day so I can see her perform live. I'm helping to arrange a meeting so Polish Swifties can join together and sing her songs and chat about Taylor. It will be a lovely day for everyone who comes. I'm really excited."Sara is eighteen and from Warsaw. Her favorite three songs are "Out Of The Woods," "I Knew You Were Trouble" and "All Too Well." She says: "My favorite video has to be *Style*. It is so magical and her love interest in the video [English actor Dominic Sherwood] reminds me of Harry Styles. I was a Haylor Shipper [the name for fans who supported their relationship] when Taylor briefly dated him in 2012 and it was a shame when they broke up.

"I love how Taylor draws on her past relationships when she's writing her songs: it makes them so authentic. I love how she is kind and polite but also witty, some of her songs are so clever. I love her smile and that she likes to talk a lot . . . She's amazing!

"I like being in a Swiftie in Poland but I would like her to grow in popularity over here so that she would be more inclined to visit us. I know she struggles to visit every country where she has fans, but hopefully she will visit here one day and I'll have the opportunity to see her perform live. In the meantime, I keep watching her performances on the Internet and the TV."

CHAPTER 23
PORTUGAL

Portuguese Swifties are desperate for Taylor to one day perform a concert in their country as they would do anything to see her sing live and have the opportunity to thank her for all she's done for them.

Taylor is a role model for so many people around the world. Back in 2012, she admitted on *Live! With Kelly*: "If you're choosing to put out music and be out there in the public, you have to be conscious of the fact that you are a part of the raising of the next generation and you do have an impact on that. So, choose your outfits and your words and your actions carefully. I think it matters. I think it really does. You can pretend it doesn't, but it does."

If she does perform a show in Portugal one day, then she'll no doubt try to speak Portuguese, as she always tries to learn at least four or five phrases in the language of the country she's visiting so she can connect with any fans in her audience who don't speak English.

If you're a Portuguese Swiftie, why not connect with other Swifties from your country by becoming a fan of Taylor Swift Portugal on Facebook? There are currently over 9,000 fans of the page.

DID YOU KNOW?

Taylor's song "How You Get the Girl," from her *1989* album, was used in an ad for Diet Coke. As well as starring herself, Taylor is joined in the commercial by her cat Olivia and lots of other cats.

Ana is seventeen and from Lisbon. She says: "It's hard to choose my favorite three, but the last three I listened to were 'Clean,' 'Back To December' and 'All Too Well.' Taylor writes amazing songs and always comes up with creative videos for them. My favorite two are *I Knew You Were Trouble* and *Back To December.*

"What I love the most about Taylor is EVERYTHING. She is ball of sunshine, she is always smiling; she cares about other people. Despite all of her success she doesn't forget where she belongs, where she came from. I love the passion she puts into her songs and in every single thing she does.

"Even though I've never met her, I feel so close to her. She's my role model. It is hard to be a fan in Portugal because she's never visited here. There aren't many Swifties in my country and I don't hold out much hope that she'll visit us, but it would be amazing if she did."

CHAPTER 24

SINGAPORE

Singapore loves Taylor Swift and she performed her first Speak Now World Tour date at the Singapore Indoor Stadium on February 9, 2011. She came back again with her Red Tour in 2014. This time it was the last show of the tour, performing at the same stadium as the previous occasion, on June 12, 2014. For the 1989 World Tour she performed two dates, on November 7 and 8, 2015.

Before Taylor took to the stage for her Red show she was presented with a platinum sales plaque for her sales in Asia. Her *Fearless* album had sold 400,000 copies in Asia as a whole, and her *Speak Now* album had gone platinum in Taiwan, South Korea, Indonesia and the Philippines.

Taylor admitted afterwards to The Associated Press: "Some of them were really surprising to me. I wasn't aware of every single certification we have in Asia. It really blew my mind.

"I love country music, and I love the fact that it's being accepted all over the world. That is so exciting for me. I have heroes who have taken country music internationally. You have Garth Brooks and Shania Twain. They really did a lot for country music because they brought an awareness of it. The fact that I have the opportunity to do that too and go to other countries where I've never been before and play music—it's what I've always dreamed of doing."

She loves performing in countries like Singapore, adding: "The international success has been the most beautiful and pleasant surprise. Being welcomed by countries that speak a different language from the language I speak is an honor.

"It really touches me every time I look down and I see all the fans singing the words to my songs, having written the lyrics, knowing that they connect in countries where English really isn't spoken by everyone. It means the world to me."

During the Asian leg of her tour Taylor had managed to find time to see some of the sights and experience Asian culture. During her trip, she visited Singapore Chinatown, dressed up as a geisha in Tokyo and visited a beach in Hong Kong.

If you're from Singapore, why not join the Taylor Swift-Singapore (Official Fan Club Page)? The page currently has more than 17,000 fans and is a great place to keep up with the latest Tay news, enter competitions and find out about fan events in your area.

DID YOU KNOW?

"Sparks Fly" was a song that had been sitting on Taylor's shelf for years until she decided to include it on her third album, *Speak Now*. Fans had fallen in love with it after hearing her sing it live.

Meris is twenty and from Singapore. Her favorite three songs are "Love Story," because it changed her life, "All Too Well" as it was the first song that made her cry and she can relate to it on a very deep level, and "Clean" because that song gets her through the toughest times and it reminds her that everything will be okay again.

Meris says: "I'm an ordinary twenty-year-old girl from a tiny country called Singapore but I have an extraordinary role model named Taylor Swift. It all started in 2009 when my sister showed me Taylor's *Love Story* music video. That was a life-changing moment because it was the moment that Taylor captured my attention and it is pretty safe to say that my life was never the same again. My sister only showed me the video because she liked the dress Taylor wears in it, but I was captivated by Taylor and have been ever since.

"What really made me become a Swiftie was her journey to success. She was determined, hard-working and, most importantly, she dared to dream. She never gave up, even though plenty of record labels rejected her when she gave them her demo CDs. Taylor wasn't a singer who rose to fame overnight through a discovery on YouTube: she went up to every record label to present her talent to them and I feel that she was very brave for doing that. This is why I relate to her. I am from a small country where the entertainment route isn't encouraged, but my dream is to become an actress. Her fearlessness to dream big and to chase the dream influences me to chase my own dream and I am so glad that throughout these years, I am definitely closer to reaching this acting dream of mine.

"Over the years, Taylor has helped me. It was always a goal of mine to thank her for all the positive impact she has made on my life because, honestly, I wouldn't be where I am today if it wasn't for her. I am extremely lucky to have been given the chance to meet her three times when she visited Singapore for the Red Tour in 2014.

"Here's how it all happened. A couple of weeks before her supposed only show in Singapore on June 12, 2014, promoters announced that Taylor would be performing in Singapore on June 9, 2014 as well, due to the cancellation of the Thailand show. Without thinking, I purchased tickets to both shows because I knew that would give me double the chance of getting a Club Red pass to meet her. Club Red is never confirmed for every show, so no one was sure if there would be a Club Red in either show in Singapore, but I was hoping there would be.

"During the couple of weeks before the shows, I worked really hard at taking part in contests held by Cornetto, AirAsia and several newspapers. My hard work paid off because I won a pair of meet-and-greet passes for the June 12 show. When I found out, I was beyond excited. I cried, I laughed, I didn't know what to do. It was so amazing to think that my dream of meeting Taylor was going to come true. It was so overwhelming. I was being given the chance to say everything I'd wanted to say to Taylor for the six years I'd been a Swiftie.

"A day before the first show in Singapore, I tried looking for Taylor, as any (obsessed and normal) Swiftie would do. I didn't manage to find Taylor, but I met her mom, Andrea, so I passed a cat cuddly toy, which had lots of hair bobbles [hair ties] attached to it. When I'd been wondering what to get

Taylor as a gift, she'd tweeted something about losing her hair bobbles in every country she goes to, so I knew my gift had to incorporate hair bobbles. I also attached a note to the gift bag that said something like, 'Here's a cat stuffed toy and some hair ties because you lose them everywhere you go, so hopefully you will never run out of them. I will be meeting you on June 12, 2014 and I will be passing a painting to you then. Can't wait! Love, Meris,' and I also included my Twitter handle, Instagram name and email, not expecting any reply in return.

"On June 9, 2014, I woke up really early in the morning because I was excited that I was finally going to watch the Red show. As usual, I checked my email and for once, an official-looking email sat in my inbox, in the midst of all the advertisement emails I usually get. I opened it and the sender was someone from AEG Live, the promoter of the Red Tour in Asia. The rest of the email refused to load and by this time, my head was pounding. Finally, the whole email loaded. I read: 'Taylor would like to invite you to the meet-and-greet this evening after receiving your gift.' WHAT?! First of all, I did not know there was a meet and greet for the June 9 show because it was a last-minute one. Secondly, TAYLOR IS INVITING ME TO MEET HER! That was not normal. I started running around the house and screaming and crying, and I literally did not know what was going on. Trust me, my sister recorded a video of my reaction and it was chaotic.

"Later that evening, I was ready to go into the meet-and-greet. I remember shaking really badly while waiting in line to say hi to the person who had changed my life since I first heard 'Love Story,' back in 2009. Obviously, I was terrified. What if she doesn't like me? What if I screw this up? I only have one go at this . . . What if I can't get any words out of my mouth? I remember that I was on the verge of hyperventilating and everyone was staring at me. Fortunately, I managed to calm myself down just before going in to meet her and went through a few points in my head on what I was going to say to her. When I met Taylor, she was genuinely interested in everything I was telling her and she was incredibly bubbly, kind and beautiful. She reminded me again why I love her so much—because of her personality and the close relationship she has with her fans. Her cheerful laughter was extremely contagious and it was such a joy to meet her for the very first time in my life. I am glad I survived that five minutes of meeting her and managed not to faint.

"During the show afterwards, I had red glowsticks around my arms and a very well-lit heart-shaped board. As one of the only people standing and awkwardly dancing in the section with my DIY Junior Jewels shirt [like the one Taylor wore in her *You Belong With Me* video] and fedora hat, I was called a lot of times by the ushers to sit down. I refused to back down, so I shifted to the aisle a lot to dance with two Swifties that I met that night. We danced and had so much fun and during the last song, 'We Are Never Getting Back Together,' Andrea came up to the three of us and asked a question that every Swiftie would want to hear in their lives: 'Do you want Club Red?' I couldn't believe it. I was going to meet Taylor again!

"Taylor might have just put on an amazing show but she still looked flawless and so beautiful when she met us backstage. Taylor was very welcoming to every Swiftie she met at

Singapore's Club Red by giving everyone a big warm hug even before saying hi. She didn't treat us as her fans: she treated us as friends.

"Taylor remembered me and when I saw her again at the meet-and-greet on June 12 she said, 'Thanks for coming again!' She really liked the cat T-shirt I was wearing and my painting. It had 'Long Live *Red* Era' on it because it was the last show and I felt it was very apt for the situation. This time around, our conversation was very casual and I honestly felt like I was talking to a friend. She was so friendly and sociable, and so witty—she has a great sense of humor.

"Through the three times of meeting her, Taylor really proved to me that I made the right decision in choosing her to be my role model in 2009. She makes an effort when it comes to connecting with us and it's a rare and beautiful thing that even though she is one of the biggest superstars out there, she is also one of the most reachable role models. It is without a doubt difficult to meet Taylor here in Singapore because of the time she spends in this country, but when we do get to meet her, she treats us the same as she treats any other person she meets in another country. Although we don't have the luxury of buying merchandise from Taylor's online store, I am very thankful that we have easy access to her albums and magazines when she is on their covers.

"Taylor has chosen to be a good role model for young children, teenagers and even adults. There are so many ways Taylor has helped change my life for the better—she's encouraged me to chase my dream, no matter how big it is, creating beautiful music that is there for me whenever I need it and inspiring me to become a better person than I ever was before, and this is just the story of one person. I have read so many stories of Taylor helping fans who are going through tough times and every single story makes me love Taylor more and more."

Nicole is fifteen and from Singapore. Her favorite songs are "Fifteen," "All You Had To Do Was Stay" and "Crazier." She can't decide what her favorite music video is because she likes *Blank Space*, *Mine* and *Begin Again* equally. She says: "Taylor really captured the emotions of the songs in these music videos; they are just perfect.

"What I love about Taylor the most is how selfless, caring and happy she is! She inspires me to be a good friend and I always try to be positive in every circumstance, just like she is.

"I really enjoy being a Singaporean Swiftie. Taylor has come here for every tour since *Speak Now*, so we're really blessed. As well as seeing her shows over here, I travel overseas too. I recently went to Philadelphia in America and Brisbane in Australia to see her perform. If I had any wish it would be that there were more Swifties in my country, but at least I can speak to fans from other countries on Twitter."

CHAPTER 25

SOUTH AFRICA

Taylor hasn't brought any of her tours to South Africa but hopefully she will one day, as South African Swifties would give anything to see her play live. They might be small in number, but they are dedicated and want Taylor to notice them one day. Why not check out their page, Taylor Swift South Africa, on Facebook?

One dedicated South African Swiftie traveled all the way to England to see Taylor perform her 1989 show but because her flight was delayed, she missed all but three songs of Taylor's Hyde Park performance. Stephanie shared how she was feeling on Twitter: "Made the last 3 songs. Plenty of tears were shed today. Absolutely broken. Horrific. Just horrific."

The next day, Taylor saw Stephanie's tweets and wanted to help her. She tweeted: "I'm really sorry you missed it but if you can get to Dublin I'll buy you tickets! Sorry to hear about the travel nightmare. :("

Stephanie managed to make it to Dublin and when she checked into her hotel for the night, she was surprised to receive two cakes, a bottle of prosecco and a message saying, "Congratulations Stephanie you made it!!! #yeswecan from fellow Swifties at the Gibson Hotel." She was really touched and had an amazing night at Tay's concert.

This isn't the only time Taylor has gone above and beyond to look after her fans. For Christmas 2014, she sent some of her biggest fans Christmas presents she'd wrapped herself and in January 2015, she paid for a fan's college fees with a check for $1,989.

Taylor might not have toured in South Africa but she did film her *Wildest Dreams* music video there. She donated the proceeds of the single to the African Parks Foundation, which was very generous of her. Some people in the press didn't like the video and negative articles appeared, but many Swifties thought it was great and that it showcased the wonderful landscape and animals of South Africa.

Not many Swifties know this but the Shelby Cobra car that Taylor attacks with a golf club in the *Blank Space* video was actually custom-made in South Africa. The car's owner, Will Hough, revealed to *The Garage* that he was impressed with the special effects and CGI used, as Taylor didn't actually smash his car up on the day they filmed. He said: "It shocked me because when I was there, it was all about her singing, chasing the boyfriend, with him laying halfway out of the car. So when the video came out, someone said to me: 'Will, I can't believe Taylor Swift smashed your car like that!'

"It didn't actually get smashed in the video at all. What happened was at the end of the video, she put her hand down and scratched up the front of the car. They paid $3,200 to have the whole car repainted, because you can't blend in on fibreglass."

DID YOU KNOW?

"Back To December" from Taylor's third album, *Speak Now*, is thought to be about her ex, *Twilight*'s Taylor Lautner, "the boy from Michigan." Taylor revealed on a post on her official website: " 'Back To December' addresses a first for me, in that I've never apologized to someone in a song before. In the good, or bad, or the apology, the person I wrote the song for deserves this. This is about somebody who was incredible to me, just perfect to me in a relationship, and I was really careless with him, so these are the words that I would say to him—that he deserves to hear."

It's thought that her track "Holy Ground," from *Red*, could also be about Taylor Lautner, or it might be about Joe Jonas.

Trisha is twenty-one and from Cape Town. She's been living in England for the last three years but visits South Africa whenever she can.

Trisha became a fan after hearing "Breathe" from Taylor's *Fearless* album. She explains: "After my dad passed on, I always listened to that song and I didn't even know who sang it. It calmed me down when I was sad, and it made me feel better. The fact that I couldn't breathe without him but I actually had to move on really resonated with me. When I found out the song was by Tay, I looked out for other songs by her and I found out she actually had REAL stuff—songs she'd written about her own life and experiences.

"Tay writes her songs from her heart and you can tell just by listening to her singing. She's extremely open about her love life and her private thoughts and feelings and she isn't afraid to express them in a song.

"If I had to choose my favorite Tay songs I would pick 'Wildest Dreams,' because it's such a calm song, 'Our Song,' 'Bad Blood' and 'Shake It Off'—they are all so different. The *Bad Blood* video is pretty unbeatable; it's awesome. I think the video for *You Belong To Me* showcases how great Tay is at acting; she pulled both roles off perfectly.

"Her songs make me feel good about who I am and inspire me to believe that I can become who I wanna be. I just have to be strong and focus on the future. I actually joined Twitter just to follow up on her and get to meet people who love her as much as I do.

"One of the things I love most about her is how generous she is. Did you know she's been named the most charitable celebrity in the world for the last three years? She always takes time out to visit sick children in hospitals, she donated all the proceeds from her single, 'Welcome To New York' to public schools in the city, she sends fans presents and cards . . . she's amazing!

"Being a fan in South Africa is kinda different from being a fan in other countries because Taylor has never been here and this means there aren't many opportunities for fans to get together. Last year, when I went back, I met three South African Swifties I had met on Twitter in Cape Town over coffee; it was lovely. We'd love it if we could go see Tay perform in Cape Town in the future."

Tatum is eighteen and from Cape Town. She says: "My favorite three songs have to be 'Shake It Off,' 'Fifteen' and 'Mean.' I love 'Shake It Off' because it's really catchy and makes me jump and dance—if I'm in public, this dancing is restricted to head bobbing and foot tapping. 'Fifteen' is special to me because I feel Taylor allowed us into parts of her childhood with this song. I like the fact that this song has meaning and it's something I would say to my younger self to avoid unnecessary heartache—don't forget to look before you fall. 'Mean' is a song for all the haters who make fun of you and knock you down with everything they have. Tay teaches us to stand up and ignore the bullies.

"My favorite music video is definitely *Shake It Off*. I love the fact that she can't dance, but she's totally fine with it and embraces it! As one who lacks rhythm, I know the struggle of not being able to just dance in public because of the humiliation that can come from doing so. I love the fact that Tay's real, genuine and truly cares for her fans. She loves and respects people. She's always smiling and happy. She gives me faith in a better tomorrow and shows me that not all celebrities are full of themselves.

"To be a fan in South Africa is really sad because kids my age don't like Taylor Swift, but that moment when you find a Swiftie, fireworks go off. Taylor has not performed here yet and it sucks big time but hopefully she will one day.

"I've never seen her in concert but I love watching as many clips on YouTube as I can. I loved that during her final

Speak Now concert in the United States she sang 'Who Says' with Selena Gomez. I also loved it when she sang 'Baby' with Justin Bieber. She's such a talented singer and her duets are epic. It's great how she surprises fans at her concerts with her special guests."

CHAPTER 26
SPAIN

Taylor brought her Speak Now Tour to Spain, performing one date at the Palacio de los Deportes in Madrid, but sadly she didn't come back with her Red or 1989 Tours. She has made brief trips to Spain but is never able to spend a long time in the country, even though she would love to.

In January 2013, she went to the 40 Principales Awards in Madrid to collect the award for Best International Artist and to perform "Love Story" and "We Are Never Ever Getting Back Together." She had a great time, dancing along to the other performances and finding out more about the Spanish music scene. To see a video of Taylor's performances, head to YouTube, where you'll also find a cute video of her speaking Spanish.

Taylor is hugely popular in Spain and the Taylor Swift Spain Facebook page has more than 33,000 fans. They regularly organize special meet-ups and events, so if you live in Spain then you should definitely join. You should also check out the fansite: www.taylorswift.es.

DID YOU KNOW?

In her bonus track, "Wonderland," from her *1989* album, Taylor references the classic book *Alice in Wonderland* by Lewis Carroll. She sings about falling down a rabbit hole with a boy and him having a Cheshire cat smile.

Paula is nineteen and from Mequinenza. She says: "Trying to choose my favorite three songs is really tough because there are so many of Tay's songs that I love. 'Never Grow Up' will always be a special song for me. I can still remember the first time I heard it, and every time I've heard it since, it still feels the same. There's just this big huge feeling of having someone who understands the feeling of moving forward as something both good and bad and knowing the risks; it's what it makes me love this song so much. It made me cry and feel that I had someone who had felt the same—it sounds cliché but it's true.

"Another song I've fallen in love with is 'Clean.' This song is about being healed by time and yourself. Listening to this track brings peace to my soul because every time I feel weak, this song tells me that time will heal me. I love 'New Romantics' and its message that the whole idea of love is a cycle that never ends and friendship is the one way of survival. Sometimes all you have to do is shake it all off and be proud of how you've felt and will feel, be fearless.

"My favorite video is *Blank Space* and my favorite album is *1989*, although I think *Red* is really special as well. If I had to choose one thing that I love about Tay the most, I'd have to say her kindness. She always tries to do good to herself and to other people. She has always let everyone know she is still learning and so are we. She has taught many of us to forgive and love ourselves.

"There aren't many Swifties in the area of Spain where I'm from, which means it can be quite isolating at times. I first became a fan after I saw her perform 'Teardrops On My Guitar' on TV. Both myself and my mom thought she was great, but my friends at school were ashamed of liking her, so treated me badly when I was open and honest about being a fan. They would gossip about me and pick on me, but I continued to be a fan of Taylor and her music.

"I'm so glad that I didn't give up supporting Taylor. Once *1989* came out, people's opinion on Taylor changed and I was no longer ridiculed for supporting her. She's growing in popularity in Spain now and I'm so proud of all that she's achieved. I really hope I get to meet her one day and tell her face-to-face how amazing she is."Alba is nineteen and from Tavernes de la Valldigna. She says: "My favorite three songs are 'Begin Again,' 'You Are In Love' and 'New Romantics.' My favorite video has to be *Style* because I love the filmography and the atmosphere in it. It's so beautiful and haunting, I just love it.

"Taylor is an artist who evolves and she wants to improve as an artist every day, which I find so inspiring. She writes wonderful songs and her voice is incredible. She is so thankful to every single fan for supporting her and she puts in so much time building relationships with fans from around the world through social media.

"Being a fan in my country is very hard. First of all, we are considered stupid little girls for loving Taylor by our friends, which I hate. And the second thing is that she rarely comes to Spain to perform, which makes me really sad because I've been dreaming to go to a Taylor Swift concert since I was, like, twelve. I really hope she decides to perform her next tour here."Isabel is twenty-three and from Barcelona. Her favorite songs are "Clean," "Tim McGraw" and "You're Beautiful." She says: "They all mean so much to me. At different times in my life each one of them has been my 'national anthem.'

"My favorite music videos at the moment are *I'm Only Me When I'm With You*, *The Best Day* and *I Knew You Were Trouble*. The first two are the ones that made me fall in love with that Tennessee girl and become not only a fan of her music, which I already was, but a fan of her and her smile and her madness. And I'm still touched by the opening monologue on the *IKYWT* video. It hurts and it heals.

"The thing I love most about her is her authenticity. She is who she says she is. A lot of people have tried to bully me for being a Swiftie. They say, 'She's a product of the music industry.' It's useless to try and argue, so I like to say that if she's a product, she's my all-time favorite product. And that's the end of the discussion.

"In my country Taylor was unknown before *1989*. As a result of this, I have been judged for calling myself a Taylor Swift fan in the past. People used to say I had bad taste in music. I couldn't afford to see her Speak Now Tour and there was no Red Tour or 1989 Tour in Spain, but I still love being a Spanish Swiftie."

CHAPTER 27

UNITED KINGDOM

Taylor absolutely loves spending time in the UK, where she has performed lots of times. She has promoted all her albums in the UK and brought all her tours there. She's lost count of how many interviews she's done for journalists and TV hosts in the UK—over the years, she's literally done hundreds and hundreds.

The UK was the only place in Europe where Taylor brought her Fearless Tour, so the fans there were very blessed to have a total of six dates. Taylor visited London, Manchester, Chelmsford and Staffordshire during her trip and had an amazing time. She was back again in March 2011, with her Speak Now Tour, and performed dates in London, Belfast, Birmingham and Manchester. For her Red World Tour, she performed four dates in London, and for her 1989 World Tour, she performed in London, Glasgow and Manchester.

Despite having many more opportunities to meet Taylor than fans from other countries, UK fans would still like to see her more because you can never get enough Tay time!

DID YOU KNOW?

In Taylor's song "Speak Now," from her third album of the same name, Taylor sings about a guy her friend had dated at school getting married to someone who treats him badly. She explained to E!News: "He had met this other girl, who was a horrible person. She made him stop talking to his friends, cut off his family ties and made him so isolated. And, randomly, I was, like, 'Oh, are you going to speak now?' "

Taylor loves sightseeing when she visits the UK and during one trip to London she went to see the sights, even though it was raining. She went for a walk in Hyde Park, spent some time at the Princess Diana Memorial, visited London Zoo and went shopping in Portobello Road, West London.

Taylor has dated two British men, One Direction's Harry Styles and DJ Calvin Harris. When she was dating Harry, they visited the Lake District together, and with Calvin, she went on an amazing boat trip on the Thames. Taylor and Calvin shared a photo of themselves on the boat with their friends, supermodels Gigi Hadid and Karlie Koss, and Joe Jonas of the Jonas Brothers. Taylor wrote: "Little-known fact: Karlie is secretly an unofficial historian/London tour guide. Kind of."

Many people believe that "I Knew You Were Trouble" from Taylor's *Red* album was based on her relationship with Harry

Styles but some Swifties think it was written well before they even started dating. When she set out to write the song, she wanted it to be "really chaotic" and "crazy." Justin Bieber absolutely loved it and thought it was the best song Taylor had done up to that point in her career.

She performed the song at the BRIT Awards, an event that Harry was attending with his band, One Direction. Taylor told reporters: "It's not hard to access that emotion when the person the song is directed at is standing by the side of the stage, watching."

Chloe is eighteen and from Southampton. Her favorite three songs are "Fifteen," "Long Live" and "All Too Well." She says: "Why I love Taylor—this is literally the hardest question because I don't know where to start! Over the past eight years she has taught me to be myself because there's no one better; that it's okay to not be okay and to keep fighting for your dreams. I thought I was invisible to her but when I met her, it made me realize that she sees everything—she's always looking out for us and supporting us. I can't think of another celebrity who loves their fans more than Taylor does—she let five hundred fans listen to the *1989* album early, she sends money to pay off college debts, she lets around thirty people meet her after nearly every concert in an exclusive hand-picked event (T-party for the Fearless Tour and Club Red for the Red Tour), she sends Christmas and Valentine's Day presents to fans, she follows and interacts with us on Tumblr (I was lucky enough to get a follow too!) etc.—the list is endless.

"Whenever I'm sad, she's there for me and whenever I'm happy, she's there for me. If we didn't fight for our dreams, she wouldn't be a multi-million dollar recording artist and I wouldn't be following my dream career path and I wouldn't have met her. She makes me want to be a better person, to follow my dreams and just enjoy my life more. I love her so much and I will support her all my life.

"I think I'm really lucky to be a fan from England—there are negatives but there are so many positives. Her music is available everywhere, she's always being played on the TV and radio, she's often on magazine covers, we get her American magazines here too; she visits numerous times a year and tours here. I feel really lucky that she loves Fundon [London] and the UK so much. However, when she tours, she only ever does about five dates in the UK. I know this is more than a lot of countries get, but I just wish she would do more tour dates because there is definitely the demand for it. In America, her merchandise is available at Target and Walmart. However, here you can only get her merchandise direct from her website in the UK. There are often Taylor competitions but they are only open for residents of America so it cuts off fans from all over the world. However, I do feel really lucky overall and I wouldn't change anything.

"I met Taylor on October 10, 2014 and this is my story. I'll start from the beginning and try to remember every last detail. Just a few days before I met her, I'd posted a photo and message on Instagram, saying how I was sure that I wasn't ever going to meet Taylor. I said that I thought that people would already have been contacted if there was going to be a London secret session and that only people who have been noticed by Taylor/ Taylor Nation get invited. Just a few days later, I got an email out of the blue from Taylor Nation—I burst into tears and ran to my mum. She instantly thought that something awful had happened and I managed to say, 'Secret sessions, read it!' The email basically said that they loved how much I support Tay on my social media and that they wanted my information. I replied immediately and waited.

"The next day I got a direct message on Twitter from Taylor Nation, which pretty much said the same thing as the email. Again, I emailed them immediately. I then got a call at 3:35 p.m. as I was walking home—I was listening to 'All Too Well' at the time. I never usually pick up the phone if I don't recognize the number but I saw 'TN, USA'—TENNESSEE = NASHVILLE = TAYLOR = TAYLOR NATION. I talked to a really lovely girl called Sierra and she said, 'Hey, is that Chloe?' in the most adorable accent EVER—I'm in love with it! Then I started crying and managed to say yes. She asked me a few questions and then she asked how big of a Taylor Swift fan I was, and I said, 'I'm currently walking along the street crying, is that enough?' and she said that I was 'so cute'! I had to write down all the information but as I was walking home I couldn't do that yet, so she chatted to me on the phone as I walked home! I literally cried during our entire conversation. Once I got home, Sierra invited me to London and I wrote down all of the information. Then she said that I could now scream and call my mum. I wasn't allowed to tell anyone apart from Mum. When I got off the phone, I just had to sit and cry and scream for a little while.

"I texted my mum and she said, 'I'm so excited I could burst and I'm not even going to meet her!' (I wasn't allowed to bring anyone with me as I'm eighteen.) I started working on a letter I could give to Taylor. I knew that I wouldn't be able to tell her anything when I met her because I'd be crying so much, so I wrote down all the most important things that I wanted her to know. I'm so glad that I did this!

"Mum and I looked at staying at Tay's hotel but the cheapest room was, like, £350 so that was out of the question! We got a really nice hotel that was only ten minutes' walk away so it worked out well. We got a lift to the station, the train and then two subways. We had to lie to my granny about where we were going and I felt so bad! (We told her afterwards and she was like, 'Taylor whatshername?' Ha ha!) So Mum walked me to the hotel and she was so nervous about letting me go, as she had no idea what would happen.

"I walked up to the hotel and nearly got run over by a taxi, but a lady that worked there luckily told me to move. Then I checked in and was taken to the room where everyone was. This hotel was literally amazing—I'd never been somewhere so posh and elaborately decorated! There were about thirty people in the room and I got in the line to check in and got chatting to some girls and their mums. Everyone was so lovely and easy to chat to—we exchanged Twitter names and loads of us already followed each other, which was crazy! I then got chatting to Shannon and her mum and they were stood behind me. Shannon's mum said that I'm very well spoken and I pronounce my words nicely—like, *What? Do I?!* Mum's happy with that compliment!

"We all chatted for a while as people signed confidentiality papers and checked their bags in. It was then my turn to check my stuff in and I told the ladies at the desk that I had a letter for Tay and they said to give it to them at the end and they would give it to her. I then had to sign some paperwork—my hands were shaking so much! I wasn't allowed to say anything about the location/track names and numbers/lyrics/Taylor's inspiration for each song/etc. She wanted *1989* to be a surprise for all of her fans, which I totally understood.

"We then all chatted in the room together for maybe another half an hour? Shannon and I got chatting to Abi and her mum. Abi looks so much like Taylor and her outfit was exactly like something that Taylor would wear! It turns out that Abi and her mum, Clare, remembered me from the Red Tour—I was so shocked. Abi was a few rows in front of me on 1 February and you can see her sign in nearly all of my photos from the tour! It was so crazy to actually hug and talk to someone that I've talked to for ages on Twitter! It turns out that a few people had seen me at the Red Tour in my purple *Speak Now* dress—HOW CRAZY IS THAT?! The cutest thing was when you told someone your Twitter username and they said, 'Oh yeah, I think I follow you!' So cool!

"So then Taylor's main security guard came in and told us that we were all special because we didn't freak out whenever Taylor tweeted, we didn't post funny photos of her and we were totally normal—ha, ha, ha, okay! Shannon and I were holding hands so tight and there was such a tense and exciting atmosphere in the room. Then people were shown through to another room in small groups. I was waiting to be called through with Abi, Beth, Hannah and Liv, and we were all stood in a circle holding hands and it was so cute and exciting!

"Just a few minutes later our names were called and we walked into the other room. One of the ladies who works for Taylor, her name was Karli, told us that Taylor handpicked us all and I lost it then. The tears started. I was sobbing and managed to say to Krissy, 'I didn't think she knew that I even existed!' and the lady that told us said that she wasn't going to tell anyone else that because of our reactions—ha, ha! Then we all pinkie promised that we'd stay in touch and it was so lovely. Then we were all checked by security and led to Taylor's room!

"So we were all walking along the corridors and in the lifts holding hands and it was like a little Swiftie support circle and everyone was so lovely. The security guy that took us up was so funny and kept joking that we were in the wrong elevator to meet Taylor and that we were meeting Justin Bieber instead, and there were other people in the elevator and they had no idea that we were meeting Taylor Swift! We went into the suite and it smelled AMAZING—there were loads of Jo Malone candles being burned! We were led down a few steps to where everyone else was and there was a table full of food. I could only manage one piece of pizza, but there was pizza, sushi, carrot sticks, tomatoes, broccoli, chicken nuggets, and that's all that I can remember!

"Only, like, ten minutes later we were brought back up the little stairs and into the lounge area. Me and Shannon were the last ones up so we were sat near the back of the room, but that was okay because I have such long legs that I fidget constantly trying to get comfy—ha, ha! The two boy Swifties were sat next to us too and Millie and Sophie. We were all chatting nervously while we were sat on the cushions on the floor and all the parents were sat on the sofas at the edge of the room.

"Then I heard, 'Hey, guys!' and Taylor was behind me! I'd been expecting her to walk out from the door behind the chair but she was behind me! She is SO TALL! I know I'm tall, but her Louboutins must have been four or five inches tall—she looked like Bambi with these huge heels on! She tiptoed her way through the crowd and sat in the chair at the front. She was wearing her Louboutins, black tights and a black skater dress that had shoulder cutouts—she looked amazing!

"Then she started talking to us and I couldn't take my eyes off her, and I was crying and just, wow, my idol was, like, ten feet away from me! Before she came in, I counted and there were twenty-one Swifties there. Only twenty-one out of the whole of the UK! (There were four secret sessions in the USA and there were usually eighty-nine people at each one!!!) She said something along the lines of, 'I've been stalking all of you online for about seven months and I've interacted with some of you, but I've been silently creeping on some of you!' I swear she looked right at me and I felt like I was gonna cry because I was so happy.

"Anyway, she was just chatting so easily to us and we were all laughing at her jokes and she said that she was gonna play us the album! She took her phone out of its case so that she could put it in the docking station, and her phone case was covered in photos of cats and someone at the front said something about it and she said, 'It's from Topshop' in the cutest way EVER. She said something in an English accent too and I literally died, she sounded so cute and posh! She started by introducing each track and saying what her inspiration was for it, and then she played the song, mouthed the lyrics and did her adorable awkward dancing! Then Tree (Tree Paine, her publicist) told her that we had to turn the volume down because they could hear it from the elevators and Taylor said that it wasn't loud enough and they went back and forth a little bit, and Taylor eventually did a puppy dog face and was like 'Maaan!'— it was so cute!

"We had a break halfway through and Tay said that she had cookies and cupcakes. We all cheered because yum and because she might have made them. Then she apologized because she hadn't been able to make them as 'There's no oven here, like, what kind of hotel doesn't have an oven?' It was so sweet and it totally didn't matter—she said they were from the Primrose Bakery and I've had things from there before! A lady handed me the tray of cookies and I had a chocolate one and it was delicious, and Taylor asked where the cookies were and I said that they were here, and she smiled so big at me! We then got passed a tray of mini cupcakes. The cookie and the cupcake were both so good. Taylor asked someone if they wanted to share half a cookie with her and I would have died if that had been me!

"Then she carried on talking to us about the album as she was eating and she was talking with her mouth full of cookie and trying to be all ladylike! She then asked for some water as she was 'feeling parched,' but she said it in literally the cutest and funniest voice ever! Then she told us about the inspiration for a song and where a particular line came from, and when she played the song, we all sang the line in the way that she had originally described it to us. She was laughing so much and at the end she said that no one else at the secret sessions had done that and she hoped that people sang it like that on tour!

"Some of the songs only had a short introduction but she talked for ages about some of them, which was incredible—she talked so easily to us and she seemed so at ease, which was amazing to see! When we finished listening to the album, she put 'Shake It Off' on and we all jumped up and danced. All the floor cushions seemed to magically disappear as people moved them for us so that we could dance. I literally can't dance, but when you're in the company of twenty Swifties and Taylor herself, it was just easy and natural. Everyone was jumping around and it was so fun. She went up to one of the boys, who was next to me during the line—'the fella over there with the hella good hair'—and she pointed at him and ruffled his hair!

"Then we all went back down to the area where the table and the food were while she talked to Tree and the other people there. We were in four groups—I was in Group Four with Millie, Krissy, Hannah and Liv—four is my lucky number, so I was happy with that! We could see Taylor meeting the first group from the bar that separated the levels. One of the Taylor Nation ladies took three group photos of us—one of us just standing in a group, another of us all doing a hand-heart and one of us all doing a shocked face. Tree was also filming and taking photos on her camera.

"Before long, there was only our group left, but I felt so calm that I thought I was going to be able to hold it together. We went up the stairs and waited along the edge of the room. Taylor was still meeting a few people and she kept running around, looking for new places that she could pose with them! With Abi, she ran down the stairs, cleared the table and lay on it—their photo was so cute!

"Then Millie was with Taylor, and Taylor was saying that she knows that people are from the UK if they spell color with a *U* but that it also means they could be from Australia. She's so cute! I was next—I hugged Krissy and then Tree was standing right by me. I asked her for a hug and then I totally lost it. I started crying and didn't stop for about two hours. Tree was so nice to me and I told her that I had written Taylor a letter and that the ladies downstairs said they'd give it to her. She said that was fine and that Taylor probably wouldn't reply as she gets so many letters but that she'd read it!

"Then it was my turn. I dropped my cardigan on the floor as I wanted to be able to hug her so hard. I could barely see her as I walked toward her because I was crying so hard. She hugged me so tight—like so, so, so tight—and she properly wrapped her arms around me. We hugged for ages, like at least thirty seconds, and then I started to let go but she kept on hugging me and that made me cry even harder and I told her that I loved her. Then she looked at me and said, 'You're not wearing any makeup! You're so beautiful!' and that made me sob because I looked a mess and Taylor freaking Swift thought that I was beautiful. WHAT?! Then I managed to say, 'You know that I exist?' and she said, 'Yessss!' in the most 'obviously, of course I do' kind of voice. I asked her how she found me and she looked at me seriously and then said, 'Twitter,' and the way she said Twitter was so cute. (I have two accounts—one is dedicated to her.) She said that it was really hard to find pictures of me and she had to search for ages—she stalked my account so bad! She said that people on Instagram always post photos, so she knows what they look like and on Tumblr they did a selfie day (I can't remember which day of the week she said now—like, Selfie Sunday or something!), so she knew what lots of those people looked like. When she talks to you, she properly looks at you—she doesn't avoid eye contact. Her eyes are so intense. She's so beautiful, so petite and she's so tall—I'm not used to having to look up to people to talk to them as I'm usually the tallest!

"Then she asked what sort of picture I wanted and shrugged because I wanted her to choose—I really, really, really wanted a picture of us hugging, though! She said, 'A hugging one? Or we could sit on the couch?' I said, 'Can we do both?' She said, 'Sure,' and led me over to the couch, and everyone that was sat there just jumped out of the way and she watched me sit down. Then she sat so close to me, swung her legs over my lap and started wrapping her arms around me. I started to hug her back and accidentally touched her boob when I was wrapping my arm around her back—oops! She hugged me so hard and we took the photo and they said it would take, like, thirty minutes to appear. We stood up and I hugged her again and said, 'Thank you for everything,' and then she said that she would be back in London soon for shows and that she'd see me soon. I said to her, 'My mum says hi!' and Taylor said, 'Tell her heeeey!'

"Then one of the Taylor Nation ladies gave me my cardigan that I'd just discarded on the floor and I was shown out of the room.

"Millie was waiting outside with her mum and I was just a mess. One of the security guards offered me a box of tissues, so I pulled one out and managed to say thank you and then he said, 'I think you need more than that!' Which was very true. I was desperate for my Polaroid to come out as I was just staring at a blue/black space at the time! I was so scared that my eyes would be shut or something! Then Krissy came out and we were shown back downstairs and into the room. We were given our bags and I gave my letter to one of the Taylor Nation ladies. Then they gave us each a goody bag and there was so much in it! (I didn't properly look at it all until I got back to my hotel.) They were asking us how our night was, and it was so surreal. Then we all said 'bye' and 'thank you' and walked out. There were people sitting having drinks and chatting and they didn't even know that Taylor was upstairs!

"I had to wait for Mum to come and get me, so Millie's mum took a photo of her, Krissy and I on our phones and we wrote down each other's Twitter names. Then Krissy left and I texted my two best friends, Vick and Hol, asking if they were awake because I was desperate to call them! Millie and her mum waited with me until Mum came, which was so kind of them. Vick replied first, so I called her and she sounded so sleepy and I said, 'Vick, I just met Taylor!' She was, like, 'What? Where are you?' I started explaining and then I was crying and she was crying. (I've known her for eight years and I've only seen her cry, like, three times.) She was being so sweet, saying how much I deserved it, and that was making me cry even more.

"Mum arrived then and I said I'd call Vick back, and I said bye to Millie and her mum. I called Vick back again and she was literally still freaking out and she was tweeting about it, and Hol was texting me, like, what is going on, ring me! Then I called Hol and she just kept saying, 'What?' to everything I said—it was not sinking in! They were two of the best phone calls that I've ever made—getting to tell my two best friends that I'd finally met my idol was amazing! My Polaroid was slowly developing and I could see the outlines of mine and Taylor's bodies and Mum said we should stand under the bus stop because there were lights there. Then I finally saw my photo with my idol and I loved it so much. I couldn't stop it looking at it. It's perfect; she's hugging me and I haven't got my eyes shut. Yay!

"Mum and I walked back to the hotel and I told her everything and looked at all the merch—a bag, three 'Shake It Off' tops, a big 2015 calendar, a little 2015 calendar and a "*1989* Secret Session UK" keyring—it must have cost over £150! My phone was going crazy as I had tweeted the photo of me and Taylor and texted the girls and my Swiftie friends. Then I FaceTimed Emily and she was so jealous but so excited and it was the most surreal FaceTime session ever!

"Then I was on Twitter/Instagram/Facebook for the next two hours. People left me the loveliest comments ever and loads of them made me cry. I couldn't keep up with my Twitter notifications, they were on twenty-plus for so long! People kept saying that I deserved it and how happy they were for me, which was so surreal. I felt so overwhelmed by how amazing and supportive our fandom is! I was far too awake and excited to sleep. How on earth do you fall asleep after you've achieved your dream?

"There are so many things I'm leaving out, but everything happened so fast. I can't believe how many lovely people I met. I talked to nearly everyone, but I really want to go to a meet-up so that I can chat to everyone properly. It's amazing to be surrounded by people who love Taylor just as much as I do. Thank you to Taylor Nation, too, for contacting me, trusting me and looking after us all so well. You're all so lovely and helpful. Those three hours that we were with Taylor were the best three hours of my life. She trusts us all so much. I thought she didn't know that I existed but she had been stalking my Twitter since February. She is just amazing and I love her even more than I did before, which I didn't think could be possible!

"Taylor, thank you for choosing me out of all of the deserving Swifties—it means more to me than you could ever know. I LOVE YOU. And thank you to my mumma, for literally 'dropping everything now' and taking me to meet my idol! You are the best."

Emily is nineteen and from Chelmsford, Essex. Her favorite three songs are "Ours," "Holy Ground" and "Tied Together With A Smile." She says: "In my country, it's become increasingly easier to be a Swiftie as now that Taylor is a pop artist, she is generally very popular and all the radio stations love playing her songs. However, it is annoying when there are so many contests related to her but you have to be American to enter them!

"The night before I was due to see Taylor perform her 1989 show in London, Taylor's management/promotional team, Taylor Nation, messaged me on Twitter, asking for my contact details. This was after Taylor had liked a photo of me and my sister on Tumblr in our costumes the day before and then earlier that day had posted a screenshot on Twitter of her camera roll with our photo saved to it!

"The person from Taylor Nation said that Taylor loved our photos and had asked to meet us that night on tour before the show, but that we couldn't tell anyone or post anything until afterwards. Hardest secret I've ever had to keep!

"We had to collect our official invite letter from the box office and then go to the meet-and-greet area. Once we'd been given our wristbands, we were taken to a room with about fifteen to twenty other fans and we got to enjoy snacks like water, pizza and cookies. Taylor was behind a curtain and each pair/group went in individually. We could all hear her and see glimpses of her as the curtain came back and forth, so we were freaking out!

"Before long, it was our turn. As the curtain was drawn back, Taylor said, 'It's the prettiest princesses in the room!!!' so excitedly and was shimmying around like she does in the *Shake It Off* video, running up to us and giving us massive hugs. We chatted about her songs and tour, and I told her how I fell over in shock when she played 'Ours' as a surprise song on the Red Tour and hurt myself, to which she pulled a cute, pouting face and laughed so sweetly. I then said how 'Clean' had changed my life and she warned me she would play that one that night, so to try not to hurt myself again! We talked about how fun tutus are to dance in, and she basically called us adorable over and over before asking to take a ballet-style posed picture with us! She hugged us once more before we went off, freaked out, and then watched the best concert I've ever seen, with the best atmosphere I've ever experienced. Anyone who knows me even a little knows how much I adore Taylor, idolizing her from the age of twelve when I heard 'Love Story' on the radio and how I begged my mum to buy me the *Fearless* album.

"Will I have the opportunity to meet Taylor again in the future? I certainly hope so!"

Jaime is nineteen and from Bournemouth, England. She says: "It's almost impossible to choose my three favorite songs, but I love 'The Best Day' because it's the song that made me a Swiftie, I love 'Fearless' because it has such an incredible message, and I love 'New Romantics' because it's so upbeat and I'm so proud of how far she's come on *1989*.

"I love Taylor for so many reasons, but the main reason is because she's introduced me to so many friends. We have meet-ups and are always talking on Twitter. She's also allowed me to meet my best friend, Kristina, who I met on Twitter and who is now my best friend in real life. We meet up often in London, go to concerts together and talk basically 24/7, and I never would have met her if it wasn't for Taylor! I also love the way Taylor treats us as friends rather than fans. On the exact one-year anniversary of me meeting her in Club Red, she followed me on Tumblr, and it just feels like she's reachable as someone to talk to, rather than just another celebrity! She treats her fans so, so well.

"I love being a Swiftie in England because Taylor loves coming here and comes here quite often, which is great. It also feels like there's a community of British Swifties. Recently, we had a Swiftie meet-up in Hyde Park and about seventy people turned up! It was so much fun!

"I was lucky enough to meet her in Club Red at the Red Tour when she came to London in February 2014. I have a fan account on Twitter (@thebesttay13) and have met many friends on there. Me and my friends Becky, Justin and Rachel decided to get tickets and go together. I was lucky enough to go to all five of her shows in London and I had spent weeks leading up to the concerts making my sign and costume. I had a light-up sign that said, 'This night is flawless' and lights on my skirt and T-shirt.

"My favorite parts of the show were the B-stage songs, where each night she'd come to the smaller stage at the back of the arena with just her guitar and would perform an acoustic surprise song. It would be different each night and it was so exciting to find out what she'd be playing. She played 'Fearless' the first night and it made me so happy because it's one of my all-time favorite songs and I never thought I'd hear it live, but I did! Also, on the final night of the London shows, I was in the pit, right next to the stage, which was amazing, and the show seemed so different up close.

"Every concert, Taylor's mum walks around, picking people to come to Club Red, and so I ran down and asked her for a photo and she said, 'I'll come back!' I didn't want to get my hopes up, but during 'Holy Ground,' the second song, Andrea came back and told us we'd be meeting Taylor. She was so friendly and when she told us we'd got Club Red, I sobbed on her shoulder in the middle of the concert!

"Later on, in Club Red, Danny from The Script, Caitlin, her fiddle player and her parents were also there, so we talked to them before it was our turn with Taylor. We talked to Taylor's mum for about twenty minutes. My friend was telling her about how she started music because of Taylor and she said how great that was. We told Andrea that we were going to all five London shows and she said, 'Well, I picked the right people for Club Red then!' I told her that 'The Best Day' is my favorite song and she told me about how it makes her cry every time.

"When Taylor got to us, she hugged us all and said hi! We got things signed and she chatted to us about Ed Sheeran and how he takes pint glasses away from pubs! We told her we'd met on Twitter because of her and I gave her my (six-page) letter! She told me she'd seen my sign from the crowd and she also told us about her next album (*1989*), which she was so excited about, and told us she'd never finished anything this quickly before! It was as if we were already best friends with her and we'd known her for ages! We spoke to her for about ten minutes and we were in Club Red for over an hour! It was the best experience of my life and I am so thankful that Andrea picked me and my friends out of 20,000 people!

"I also met Taylor when she was in London for the Brits in February 2015. I camped out on the street for a total of sixty-two hours that week with all my friends from Twitter! We camped outside BBC Radio 1 because she was on the radio with Ed Sheeran. Although it was a short meeting, I managed to give her another letter and she signed my Club Red photo.

"Me and my friends also went to see her 1989 Tour in Manchester and Hyde Park, London. We dressed up in costumes and then posted photos online. During the show in Manchester, Taylor started pointing right at us and waving, then she said: 'I saw you online!' After the show, she went onto Tumblr and reblogged my post. She said: 'Did you see me point at you and say, "I saw you online" during "Love Story??" ' Course I did. Taylor had seen our photos online and recognized us in the crowd, and then after the show she had taken the time to write to us on Tumblr! At the next show in Hyde Park, we were front row and she recognized us again and said, 'I love you guys!'

"Meeting Taylor so many times has been amazing and I can't wait to meet her again—I'm a Swiftie forever!"Amy is fifteen and from Surrey, England. Her favorite songs are "Enchanted," "The Lucky One," "Dear John" and "Tied Together With A Smile." She says: "My favorite music video is probably *Everything Has Changed* because the story is so cute and I love the song! I also love *Blank Space* because I thought it was funny seeing her like the press describe her as a 'serial dater,' also Olivia Benson was a great actress!

"I love how Taylor is so open with fans and does everything for our benefit. I think it's great how she interacts with us over social media and does her best to meet as many people as she can and tour in as many countries as she can. I love how she's always positive about everything and is always smiling and laughing. I'm so proud to be a Swiftie! (Also, Olivia Benson and Meredith Grey are super cute—I love cats too!)

"Where I live, I don't really know many Swifties or go to many of her events (as there was only one near me this year) but I do fangirl a lot with my friends Livvy and Morgan—we're huge fans! I have all five of her albums and love singing along with my friends, especially songs from her early albums.

I don't really have a favorite album. I think they all go together really well and different songs go with different moods. *1989* has good songs to sing with friends and dance to, whereas *Speak Now* has more of a chilled vibe. I like how different her albums sound, but that they are always true to how she was feeling at the time she was recording them. All of the albums are amazing—there's not a song I don't like on any of them.

"I've seen Tay perform live twice. I went to see her perform at Hyde Park British Summer Time in June 2015 with three of my friends, as she was headlining. She was amazing and it was definitely the best night of my life. I also saw her at Capital's Summertime Ball in 2013 (where she performed with Ed Sheeran) and she was incredible! Ed surprised everyone when he came out onstage with his guitar to sing their song, 'Everything has Changed.' The crowd went wild and everyone sang along. I was so shocked and excited as it was my favorite song at the time; both Tay and Ed were amazing! Taylor wore her usual black high-waisted shorts with a white blouse and black flats and, of course, red lipstick. She looked gorgeous!"

Megan is seventeen and from Liverpool, England. Her favorite songs are "I Know Places," "Haunted" and "Clean." She says: "Sometimes you find a song and every single line fits into your life so easily, or you've thought those words before, and when I came across these three songs, they gave me chills and I was able to pinpoint each line of these songs with my life. My favorite music video is *Blank Space*, simply because it is so brilliant. Taylor being able to take what the media has said about her and twist it into this video is freaking amazing!

"What I love about Taylor is how genuine she is. I love that she cares about every single fan, even if she hasn't met them. Her relationship with her fans is extraordinary. I don't know any other artist who has such a busy schedule, yet manages to invite her fans to her house to listen to her album early, and offers fans free meet and greets before and after shows, and sends gifts to her fans and follows them on Tumblr and answers their questions and offers them advice. I love that even though there are millions of Swifties, your own relationship with Taylor is so genuine and personal: you find the songs that you need, and you feel that she wrote them for you. She is there in your darkest times and she helps you through it.

"I'm very fortunate to be a fan in my country, there are chances to see her live at concerts and some competitions you can enter. You can buy merchandise and it's really easy to meet up with other fans. I'm very fortunate and very grateful.

"I met Taylor Swift on June 24, 2015. Five days before her concert, I posted some pictures of my costume to Tumblr. I tagged Taylor Swift and, with the help of my friends on Tumblr and Twitter, the night before my concert Taylor liked my post. I didn't expect anything to come of it, but I was extremely happy that she had seen the effort I had gone to. Later that night I got an inbox from her Tumblr, asking for me to send some information to an email address. I did what I was told and the next day, five hours before the concert, Taylor Nation called to invite me to meet Taylor that night.

"I was so excited when I arrived at the stadium and found that my Twitter friend Ben had also been given a meet-and-greet pass. As I walked behind the curtain to meet Taylor, she shouted out, 'Oh hi, Megan! You look so cute tonight!' I was amazed that she knew my name. I was so awestruck that I almost left without collecting her autograph.

"Afterwards, me and Ben hugged each other and began crying with happiness. Even when I was watching the concert later, I couldn't help crying again because it was the best night of my life. You meet Taylor when you need her most, I cannot stress this enough."

Caitlin is sixteen and from Birmingham. Her favorite three songs are "Wildest Dreams," "Enchanted" and "All Too Well." Her favorite video is *Style* because she loves how all the graphics come together to make a refreshingly artistic video. She says: "What I love most about Taylor is that her lyrics are so carefully written and beautifully describe relatable situations. I think she goes against the typical pop industry artist and makes great songs that have depth rather than just another meaningless song. She is also so attentive to fans and has a lovable personality. She promotes being a strong female and not worrying about small things, like friendship issues.

"Being a Swiftie in the UK is great as, although there aren't many concerts she does near me, I love making trips to London to see her and the shows there are always so incredibly special, with guests such as Ed Sheeran and Cara Delevingne on the two occasions I have been, which makes the nights perfect. The volume of Swifties in one place is also magical, or 'romantic' as Taylor prefers to say.

"The concerts are so memorable because Taylor pays so much attention to the details; she has the best stage outfits, cute introductory videos of her friends and cats that make the audience laugh, and always has speeches prepared, which connect to fans individually, although there are 64,999 more than you. I love how her concerts unite Swifties and are an opportunity to dance and sing as loud as you can and be sure that everyone else is doing the same. The setlists are incredible; there's incredible dance routines and stage lifts.

"My favorite moments from the 1989 Tour in Hyde Park include the performance of my two favorite songs together ('Enchanted' and 'Wildest Dreams'), which was magical. She wore a golden dress that transformed into a jumpsuit as she rose from the piano—it was spectacular. I also remember vividly her singing 'You Are In Love' as the whole crowd was united in echoing the chorus, which was beautiful. Other key moments were the speech that preceded 'Clean' and, similarly, the art on the screen during this song and 'Out Of The Woods.' Further details include the wristbands that made a crowd of 65,000 in Hyde Park light up. Finally, as many will be aware, during 'Style' Taylor invited guests such as Karlie Kloss, Cara Delevingne and Kendall Jenner to the stage, which surely has to make a top moment! I also adored her Zuhair Murad bodysuit, as he's a favorite designer of mine. To summarize, the central aspect to Taylor's concerts is the beauty of the details."

Olivia is fifteen and from Surrey. Her three favorite songs are "Fearless," "Enchanted" and "Wildest Dreams." She says: "I discovered *Fearless* after a family friend went to Taylor's concert and shared her experience. I then became obsessed with that album and remember dancing and singing along in my room on the old CD player. At the time I would've been about eight or nine. I've been a fan ever since.

"Tay is so genuine and really tries to connect with her fans. She's really active on social media and so many Swifties have had the chance to communicate and even meet her. (I can dream!) Moreover, she is beautiful, her legs are flawless and she loves cats—Meredith and Olivia are so cute. I'm a very proud Swiftie to share my name with one of her cats.

"Being a fan in the UK is pretty amazing because her shows always come here and living so close to London means I'll be able to go to even more in the future. I was so happy when I got tickets to her 1989 Tour show in Hyde Park. It was amazing! I went with my friends Caitlin, Olivia and Amy and we had a great time. Taylor is such an amazing performer and really gets the crowd involved, plus we were given light-up wristbands to make the event even cooler!

"Taylor changed outfits so often it was hard to keep up! All her outfits were sparkly and mainly consisted of cropped bandeau-style tops and high-waisted shorts. Her outfits had to be comfortable and practical as she was dancing around the stage so much. My favorite was her white crop top and shorts, she looked flawless in it. Obviously, every outfit was topped off with red lipstick.

"In between songs at her concert, there were clips shown of her friends, including Cara and Selena, talking about Taylor, and among them were clips of Meredith and Olivia, to which the whole crowed went 'Ah!' I love how much she adores her cats. I love reading her cat tweets and that her favorite Internet meme is of a cat with the caption '*heavy breathing*.' It shows us that Taylor is just like the rest of us.

"My favorite song Taylor performed that night has to be 'Shake It Off.' It was the last song of the set, at about ten